CLEAVE

New Writing by Women in Scotland

edited by

Sharon Blackie

Published by Two Ravens Press Ltd.
Green Willow Croft
Rhiroy
Lochbroom
Ullapool
Ross-shire IV23 2SF

www.tworavenspress.com

For copyright of contributors, see page 267.

ISBN: 978-1-906120-28-3

British Library Cataloguing in Publication Data: a CIP record for this book can be obtained from the British Library.

Designed and typeset in Sabon by Two Ravens Press.
Cover design by David Knowles and Sharon Blackie. Front cover image © photographer: Michael Studard; agency: Dreamstime.

Printed on Forest Stewardship Council-certified paper by Antony Rowe Ltd, Chippenham.

About the Editor

Sharon Blackie's roots are in the north-east of England and in Edinburgh, though she has travelled all over the world and lived in France, Ireland and America. She is now firmly attached to a lochside croft in the north-west Highlands of Scotland, where she lives with her husband and a growing collection of livestock. Originally trained as a neuroscientist, she has worked in a variety of corporate consultancy roles and practised as a therapist. After completing an MA in Creative Writing at Manchester Metropolitan University, she set up Two Ravens Press with her husband, David Knowles, in 2006.

Sharon is co-editor of *Riptide: New Writing from the Highlands and Islands* (Two Ravens Press, 2007) and author of the novel *The Long Delirious Burning Blue* (Two Ravens Press, 2008). She translated from the French *The Sam Book,* a memoir of and tribute to his friend Samuel Beckett by acclaimed Franco-American author Raymond Federman.

For more information about the contributors to this volume, see
www.tworavenspress.com

Introduction

The production of a volume of collected writings by women always has the potential to be seen as a political statement, but that isn't the purpose of publishing *Cleave*. The inspiration for this anthology was quite simple: to show and to celebrate the diversity of voices of women writers who live in or in some other way 'belong to' Scotland, in 2008.

That there is diversity here should be apparent to the reader. There is for sure a diversity of origin – there are contributors to *Cleave* who were born in Scotland and who have lived here all their lives; contributors who were born in Scotland and have since moved away; contributors who are incomers, either from the rest of the UK or very much farther afield, and contributors who have lived here just for portions of their lives, but who have been influenced by that time in some deep and lasting way. Susan Sellers' essay therefore seemed to ask the perfect closing question for this book: 'Scottish? What's That?'

There is also, intentionally, a diversity of form. I wanted to include work that represented a variety of genres: short stories, poems, essays, non-fiction. The one thing I asked of all contributors was that what they offered up for *Cleave* should in some way reflect the experience of being a woman in contemporary Scotland.

Every contributor to *Cleave* has provided a 'biography' which is included in the text, just before their work. I asked for more than just a series of biographical facts – rather, that it should say something about their relationship to Scotland, something about being a woman *writer* in contemporary Scotland. (Unless, of course, this was the specific subject of their contribution.) Here, too, the diversity of approaches will be apparent, and I chose not to try to impose conformity. But in encouraging this level of personal expression it was always my hope that *Cleave* would not only provide enjoyment to its readers, but also would serve as some kind of record: a record of what it is to be a woman in Scotland in 2008.

Sharon Blackie
Ullapool, January 2008

Contents

Kirsty Gunn and Meaghan Delahunt

Kirsty Gunn is Professor of Creative Writing at the University of Dundee, where she has established her own quite distinctive undergraduate and postgraduate Modules in Writing Study and Practice. Her approach to teaching writing is based on intensive four-hour workshops which, she believes, engenders and sustains an atmosphere of intense creativity that helps individual writers find their own distinctive "voice". Once you have that, she says, everything else may follow. She has published four novels, a collection of short stories and a book of essays, short fiction and poems. Her most recent book *The Boy and the Sea* was the winner of the Sundial Scottish Arts Council Book of the Year, 2007.

Meaghan Delahunt was born in Melbourne and has lived in Edinburgh for sixteen years (on and off). Her first novel *In the Blue House* was nominated for the Orange Prize, won the Saltire First Book Prize, a Scottish Arts Council Book of the Year and a regional Commonwealth Prize. Her new novel, *The Red Book*, was published by Granta in March 2008. She is a Lecturer in Creative Writing at the University of St Andrews.

Train Notes 2007
Edinburgh–Leuchars–Dundee

Kirsty Gunn and Meaghan Delahunt often travel by train to Dundee and Leuchars (St Andrews) where they teach creative writing. The following piece grew out of their time together on that train.

Kirsty: Our conversations. Written. Spoken. There are these bits of information scattered, ideas quickly spilt. Crazy half-spelled texts and messages on each others machines. Yet… They all add up, in my mind, to a piece of writing, like the dialogue itself comes to be a kind of text. It could be something we can refer to, use. Maybe, you know, we could try and make a piece for this book in the way of a dialogue, a conversation…

Meaghan: A conversation about writing. I always love reading about the process, what writers themselves have to say…

Kirsty: So do I! Would we be the only ones?

[laughter]

Meaghan: Maybe. But okay, if we're to plunge into our writing lives like this I think I might refer to my train notebooks. I keep them in my bag for those times on the way to St Andrews when I'm not reading student work, or editing my own stuff, or reading other things, or doing my Greek homework… The thoughts that come when travelling, when in motion, are so different from the thoughts put down in a notebook before sleep. But – you don't keep any kind of journal or notebook, do you? I find that fascinating … how do you deal with day-to-day emotions in addition to writing fragments? Do you store it all up in your imagination for later? Like a Renaissance mind-palace? Rooms and rooms of thought…

Kirsty: No, I don't keep journals or a writing notebook – I never have. I remember when I was a teenager absolutely devouring anything of that sort – those Sylvia Plath journals, reading them alongside the poems and stories and her letters home to her mother… Wow. All that stuff blew my mind… That seemed to me to be the real writer's life, to write about your life while you're writing. It still does… But no. I just don't do it. I can't. I'm weirdly superstitious about it, actually. I think I would write myself out of my stories, would write myself away from them, I mean. Also, I think I'd get a bit bored. Hearing myself go on and on… I love your idea of me roaming about in some palace loaded with ideas, though… But in fact, the bottom line is that, for me, the writing comes out of some deeply interior, unknown place… More like a cave than a palace. There are no cultural reference points for it at all, the writing, in the first instance… The writing itself is the process of coming up with metaphors, meanings, a story and so on…

Meaghan: The cave. Yes. Underground. Mining the word seams, looking for light… Well, here's something from one of my train notebooks, and really, what you say, what I'm saying … whether or not one writes it down, it amounts to the same thing… The beginning of thought, imagination, conversation…

Kirsty: And I love the way you have the actual notes there to get us started!

Meaghan: So here we are. The Edinburgh – Leuchars train. Monday 8th October:

> This morning on the 9.06 the sea was glistening. This evening, coming back, the air was still soft and warm and sunny as we expressed through Markinch and Aberdour and I had one of those dislocations I have sometimes, which afflict me in autumn and spring in Scotland when it is unseasonably warm and light (rare) but it throws me off-balance and I get the seasons mixed up – or, rather, I start to experience the seasons in a visceral way as if I still lived in Australia, even after all these years, and so, for a moment this morning I thought, 'This is Spring!' because the jasmine had late-flowered outside our back door and

> the air was so inviting. Sometimes this happens in March and April when there is a chill in the air and a gold-pink light over the Crags and I think, 'This is autumn…'

Kirsty: The seasons here … as you know, I take the train, too, early. The train to Dundee. I love it, especially in the winter when it's dark and it's like I'm sitting there in the carriage in the middle of the night, still dreaming – or, like you, full of the book or story I'm working on, accompanying it on this journey. Because our stories really do travel with us, don't they? And our thoughts about our stories, other people's stories… We talk about this on the train, the days when we meet, rushed and startled out of sleep into these great and very personal discussions about writing and stories. They become our companions on the train. And outside the windows, dawn is breaking. Or, in summer or spring the light is all over the fields, and the trees stand about, startled somehow, by their own beautiful new bright green foliage, and there are the hills in the distance drawing me into thoughts about holidays and walking and an endless sense of time … and still it's all stories, stories… How we make them, how we feel about them…

Meaghan: Yes. The train is a good place to start. Let's keep our thinking to these journeys, the stories they give rise to… Together, or apart… Like there I was, it was another Monday morning (October 15) and I was suffering the kind of exhaustion which only comes from being up all night tending to a manuscript or a small child. The sense of something 'other' demanding attention. I'd planned to leave the house an hour earlier but got up late and stumbled about. Couldn't get my thoughts straight or choose what to wear or even decide whether I had to go in to work today (I didn't have to. An unnecessary train journey. I'd got my dates wrong).

I had a disturbed night because I'd started work late on the final proofs of my manuscript, after postponing and procrastinating all week. I'd circumnavigated the book as if it were a wild animal. It was as if, all week, I'd had to build up courage and strength and then somehow outwit the animal and wrestle it to the ground when it was off-guard. So strange, these fears. Why is it always like this? Much worse with a novel than with a short story, for example, but a similar process. There is nothing for it but to circle myself, this writing-self who I fear will have let me down on the page, who will have fallen far short of perfection…

Kirsty: But you know, that word you just used: "perfection". That word. That we're always setting our work up against that standard: Perfection. Maybe if I did keep a notebook I wouldn't get so bent out of shape. Because in a notebook I'd be able to confront my writing process as a day-to-day thing – and, like all day-to-day activities that are freaked by stuff that happens, random events, unforeseen circumstances that day-to-day would undermine that idea of perfection … I would see my work in that context of the real. Instead, it exists in this imagined space. The work sitting there in my mind as this perfectly conceived and realised piece of fiction. It's even a physical thing – a kind of stinging feeling of the work being complete. At some point or other I have that feeling…

Meaghan: Stinging? I love that. And then?

Kirsty: Well…

[much laughter, on and off the page]

You know…

Meaghan: Oh, yes … I know all right.

Kirsty: Because then it all goes crazy again… I don't know anything any more… It's like starting again…

And I don't know why I keep going back to my perfect, still stinging ideal – because, of course, the whole process of making a story, a book, is completely organic, I'm opening the thing up to see where it will take me… The writing is far too "live", somehow, to be perfect… So: Perfection. That word. Actually, it's a word that works much better for, say, the view from my train window this morning, on my way to Dundee. We'd diverted through Perth and there was the Tay lying along outside the train tracks in this great gorgeous thick slip of early morning light…

November and it's so golden all around me, it's like September. The light on the water reminded me of the 19th Century Russian landscapes with their lovely slabs of silver gold water, amidst the black of tree trunks and the dark blue of shadows, grasses… Do you know those paintings? Well that's perfection. But then look what I just did, there, see? Reality becoming art, again. There's no getting away from it. There's the view outside the window and it turns me straight back to the idea of making art! And how hard it is, Meaghan. Because there's the view. The thing. The idea of our work. The perfection of it. And there's the actual work. And making it, polishing it, seeing it through…

Meaghan: Not sure that I do know those paintings, but I know the sound of them, for sure … a siren song of perfection… It's the gap between what we're trying to achieve and what we actually manage… I don't know about you, but it's as if I can only look at my 'finished' work with one hand shielding my face and one eye closed, taking the measure of myself and the words, bracing myself for the worst…

Kirsty: And I see you now, doing that – shielding your hand against the bright river-y light of your work, the sun glancing off the page…

[laughter]

Meaghan: Such a hard-won process, isn't it? Then there is also that real writerly amnesia. I think all writers have a version of it? I hardly remember anything of what I've written after it's done – I guess this is how I can keep writing. In the way that women eventually 'forget' the pain of childbirth (not all women, not always) and then go on to give birth again. My process is something like that, especially with novels. It makes my editor laugh. She thinks it strange that I can't remember. I forget, and then I doubt everything. 'When a writer loses her self-doubt, she is lost,' Colette once said. But a little less self-doubt would be good…

Kirsty: Oh, yes! Forgetting. But it's a weird forgetting, too, with babies and books. Because it's not like a blank space – where the memory should be. I certainly remember: That was painful! Giving birth to Millie and then Katherine, and that was painful, too, going through the final drafts of *The Boy and the Sea*. I called you, remember, during that time, in a state – and you told me about Virginia Woolf and breaking the tablets ... It was like a cold compress ...

Meaghan: I wish I could remember that quote ... I wonder what I was reading at the time? Maybe something like: "Beauty must be broken daily to remain beautiful" (from *The Waves*). I wonder if the 'breaking of tablets' is your own? What you made of it? What you needed to hear? Your own imagination riffing on the line ...

Kirsty: Maybe. I do that all the time, I think. For years I had this thing about Natasha in *War and Peace* (I even used to tell everyone about it!) after she's met Prince Andrei at a ball ... And she's leaning her thin arms out the window (there was definitely this intense memory of reading about her thin, girlish arms) while she's dreaming about him. You know, her thin arms out in the dark summer night ... I loved that scene. Then I read the book again (I'm always reading this book – this was the third time) and it was nothing like that ... Nothing about her putting her arms out the window at all! Maybe if I kept a diary I'd be more precise about these things. But I quite like getting it all mixed up. I'll ask my friend Jane Goldman about those Virginia Woolf tablets. She'll know.

Actually, all in all, Virginia Woolf is on the train with us quite a lot, isn't she? And Katherine Mansfield. Not to mention all the Americans. And Hemingway ...

Meaghan: Oh he's with us a lot. And the Russians ...

Kirsty: They love the view ...

[At this point, Tolstoy and Turgenev join in. Hemingway spots a flock of ducks outside the train window. Instinctively, he raises

the rifle that's been lying across his lap ...]

Meaghan: Yeah, and we can forgive the machismo for just one hour of being in Old Havana drinking Cuba Libres with Papa. He reads to us from *A Clean Well-Lighted Place* or *The Old Man and the Sea* or *Hills like White Elephants* ... and, on some level, we would've loved to share a drink with the old boy. Even Martha Gellhorn was charmed (for a while). And while I'm on the subject of drink ...

The other day a very drunk Irishman sat down next to me on the train. He was sitting opposite an old friend of his from University – a beautiful British Asian woman with a London accent. He described a wedding he'd been to on the weekend. He was still steaming, and he stank, the booze sweating through his skin. He was clutching a half-bottle of Irn-Bru. He told the English woman opposite about the one time he'd ever in his life proposed to a girl and how she took an overdose shortly after. He'd walked into the hotel room, he said, and there she was on the floor, with the pills, and she'd looked up and said to him: 'I can't even kill myself properly.' He knew at that moment that it couldn't last.

This Irish boy now lived in Seattle, some big research job. He'd recently finished his PhD. This boy and the woman were both sitting on my bad ear and I would've given the game away if I turned my head or asked to swap seats just so I could hear them properly. (Many times, being half-deaf is a pain in the arse.) Anyway ... the Irishman said that he was so hammered that he'd bought a first-class ticket to Leuchars by mistake. 'But at least I got a free coffee,' he said. Then he wandered back up to the First Class carriage but was lonely without an audience and wandered back. The woman opposite was too polite (aren't we all?) to say that she wanted to get back to proofing her thesis (which is what she was doing before he sat down). And so he sat next to me again and regaled us all (unwittingly) with his tales of weight loss and weight gain and of women won and lost. 'I'm at the stage of my life' (he looked about twenty-five) 'where I'm just waiting for someone amazing,' he said. 'I went through a stage where every girl I met just loved my chat.' The woman opposite nodded and smiled encouragement. 'But lately,' he said, 'it's all dried up.' He sighed. 'These things come in waves.' His friend made soothing noises, *Of course he would attract women once again, it was only a matter of time …*

Kirsty: You've just made a short story, telling me that. It's a Hemingway moment you've just described. And all from the train …

Meaghan: Maybe. But it struck me afterwards: I hadn't heard anything from the woman opposite, who was listening to this conversation, that the man hadn't really asked her a true question since he wandered up the train and saw her sitting there. Instead, she'd played the foil to his anecdotes: encouraged him, soothed him, made him feel good about himself. He was charming, for sure, in that funny-man kind of way, and I'm sure women *do* fall for him. But it got me thinking about how often women do that thing for men, how few real questions most men ask most women. It gets me back to Virginia's famous line, 'Women reflect men back at twice their natural size.' At least, I think it was Virginia …

Kirsty: Oh wonderful! Virginia Woolf has just come back into the train, I mean. Of course she was always here …

Meaghan: But she saw the refreshment trolley …

Kirsty: She wanted a herbal tea … then she bumped into Hemingway. They had a quick vibe about form and the unconscious …

Meaghan: Exactly.

Kirsty: And now she's reminding me to ask you about this extra perspective to your story … This woman …

Meaghan: Uh-huh. Because, listening in to the conversation, I felt I knew the guy by the time we all got off at Leuchars – his job prospects, his love-life, his views on the U.S., his family, his friends. Yet I knew nothing of the woman, because he'd asked nothing of her other than to keep the conversation going, which she had, very skilfully …

Kirsty: That's a really terrific story, Meaghan. So what we have – we have Ernest Hemingway meets Virginia Woolf –

Meaghan: On the train.

Kirsty: On the train – and out of that we have this new kind of story, which is about its style, yes, the way it's told, the details – the things we see and hear while we're sitting here on the train … But then there's also the *sense* of the story, its sensibility, I mean, its interior – which is your take on the story, and, with thanks to Virginia, I think we can say it's a very organic, open-ended, female kind of take on narrative … You know, that way she and Mansfield introduce us to the kind of narrator who's not entirely sure, actually, what's going on, who asks questions, opens things up a bit, and looks, queries …

Meaghan: Well … yes. That opening up. So inspiring … I was listening, reporting back to myself … that sense the writer has of living twice – how fortunate we are, to be able to simultaneously experience and then shape through writing and the imagination. That old Henry James quote that I love: 'The glimpse became the impression and the impression became experience.' But I was also considering these other things …

Kirsty: And who was she, that woman, apart from just being a person who asked about, who made possible a male character, if you like. As the journey goes on, we start to ask these things … The journey is the writing, the writing is the journey. Both things come together again.

Meaghan: I wonder if you could say more … it's so interesting … the idea of the women character as foil for the main action. 'Men act and women appear' (John Berger). Y'know, I'd always thought of it with film. The anonymous 'girl' advancing the man's journey … But what a great point you've just made about fiction … It's actually shaken me up …

Kirsty: You know, Katherine Mansfield does a gorgeous thing with this in *At the Bay*. She has this houseful of women and children, all moving around each other, coming in and out of each other's stories... It's a beautifully fluid, organic piece of writing... And then this man appears, Stanley Burrell, the patriarch, interrupting the flow of their lives, conversations, *demanding* to be seen, noticed, responded to ... And the women do what's necessary to placate him... But, ah! The relief when he's gone! There's a beautiful sort of emptiness, a silence... In the text, after he's gone. And everything in the story happens in that space...

Meaghan: Spaces, yes. Everything happens in the places in-between. Katherine M. is very good like that. I think what distinguishes one writer from another is often that quality – that, and the breath. The intake and exhalation. Leaving room for the reader, being comfortable enough to let the space do the talking.

Kirsty: Like the space outside the train window ... we live it, we experience it, we make it into something else...

Meaghan: All this talk of making ... what about finishing? What happens for you at the end of a project? I seem to fill the immediate aftermath of a book with accidents, broken bones, surgery, illness and intimations of death. It's as if I can't quite trust that the process I've cleaved to for so long is over (at least for the time being). I fear to luxuriate in the feeling of having "finished." I think perhaps this time it's been more acute because the process of *The Red Book* has been such a long one.

Kirsty: And those feelings, as you describe, that physical effect of writing, over a long period of time, and then to "finish" ... I mean, what is finish? That image of the tide, coming in, going out outside the train window... Emptiness then the flood... A metaphor for creative process. For how can there be any such thing as "finish" ...? Yet there comes a time, of course, when we're no longer working on the piece we've been working on, the publisher has it, or your agent, whatever. Then, it's finished, I suppose. Isn't it? That thing of realising you're no longer pulling up the file out of your computer every day... That feeling...

When I start a project, when I'm in the world, with my daughters and my husband and friends, and my colleagues at University and my students ... at that point, while the project is faint, it's kind of in the distance, I'm strong in the world, I'm very much functioning out there, professionally, emotionally. But then as the story takes hold it becomes stronger and I feel myself weakening in the world by contrast, as the inner imaginative life becomes the stronger, the more real and I'm living in there, responding to its stimuli... Fading away in the other, real world – while the life of the book has become real.

Meaghan: That notion of the parallel world a writer inhabits, it's so true. The notion of many 'real' worlds. The imaginative world is as real as the sensory, material world, we have to slide and shape-shift between them... I feel, though, that with this last novel that I was utterly lost. Lost for seven years. Unable to move between worlds...

Kirsty: And to be lost is to be vulnerable. But doesn't that make just the most interesting kind of work?

Meaghan: In the long run, I think so. I hope so. It's just a hell of a toll ... The process makes you vulnerable. And you want to resist that vulnerability with control – which is the reason students and writing courses focus so heavily on the 'mechanics' of writing – plot, character, narrative arcs, conflict – all that old malarkey. As if all of these things add up to a work of art? It gives the illusion of total control. But a novel is not a machine. I can't write like that. As Grace Paley says, 'Plot the great contrivance...' or Virginia, again: 'I write to a rhythm, not to a plot.'

Kirsty: It's our train again, our journey. That coming together of art and life, the writing coming from the actual transition of one to the other. Following intuition and the sentence wherever it might lead ... And you know, when I think about it, my books are full of journeys – I mean, literally. People in cars going from one place to another. But now we've got a train, too. I love that.

There's you and me on the train – Women on a Train! Subversion! I love that idea, finding a new meaning for a metaphor that's always had such masculine connotations – linearity, climax, destination, not the spiral or the circle or the fragment ... not the way we make stories at all ... Not *Strangers on a Train* but *Writers on a Train*. Or *Writing on a Train*.

Meaghan: Train of Thought. Actually, Kirsty – I remember this was yours!

Kirsty: [laughs] Was it?

Meaghan: Yep.

Kirsty: And as I look out of the window now ... the light ... let me tell you ...

Meaghan: Yes. And the sea, always changing ... just perfect ...

Pamela Beasant

I grew up on the south side of Glasgow and went to a girls' school in the West End. Every morning I walked to the underground past the Rangers football ground, wearing a green uniform, and local kids regularly shouted 'Catholic' (which I thought quite exotic as my family were Baptists), or 'posh'. I think I always felt I wasn't a proper Glaswegian, and couldn't wait to get out of the city. I went to Oxford University, to the last all-female college, and had a brilliant time, though it was never really part of my plan to go there, and the place always seemed interestingly alien. I felt very Scottish, for the first time.

After this exclusively female education I worked in London, writing information books for children. It was a great way to train, producing tight captions that explained an electronic circuit, or how the body works. I met my husband there and we moved to Orkney, not expecting to survive as freelancers. Twenty-odd years and two children later, I still feel like an incomer – though happily so. In 2007 I was awarded the first George Mackay Brown writing fellowship, and represented Orkney elsewhere, sometimes introduced as an islander. I always pointed out that I couldn't claim Orcadian-ness, and a strange new Glaswegian sense of identity crept in. It's funny how things work out. For someone who's always felt as if I don't quite fit anywhere, the roots, both adopted and natural, have turned out to be strong. Everyone's experience of being a Scottish woman, or a woman in Scotland, is different and more or less important or meaningful to them. It's taken a long time for me to realise that it's all relative, that other people's definitions and assumptions are often wrong, and to define it for myself, and be glad of it.

Pamela Beasant

A Glaswegian in Orkney

How come they're no' understandin' the patter?
I mean tae say, for gawd's sake,
ah'm speakin' my best Kelvinside –
and they come away wi' words like
'peedie' for wee, and 'bruck' for rubbish,
and someone even says tae me
'yer no' witty' – and I wis affronted,
thinking my wee joke wisny funny,
then found out they thocht I wis a *tube*.
I nearly gave them a Glesga kiss for that.

It's no' jist the lingo, the whole place is like
flat so ye think ye'd go mental jist lookin'
at sky, and sea, and mair sky. How do the
weans – ah mean the *bairns* – survive?
Ye'd think they'd drap right aff the edge
and there's nothing tae dae, cept creep round
wee stone hooses, and rings o' bloody
monoliths that wid scare the shit oot o' ye.

Mind you – ye get a grand feed at the b&b –
and when I telt the wummin a' about the city
she says, aye, she'd been to uni there.
Turns oot she's written something that was
on the telly. Ah'm impressed, ah says,
oh really, she says, in her funny wee
sing-song voice. Ye think we're a' stupit here?
Naw, naw, I says quickly, but she's smilin'.

Ye'll tak a bere bannock? she says.
Oh aye, I says, wondering what in the
name o' the wee man she's goin' tae dae to me noo –
but willing to find out – and she plonks a brown thing,
like a tattie scone, on my plate. Oh, I says, and eats it.
It tastes like shite, but ah'm too polite to say,
being well brought up, like.

Pamela Beasant

North Ronaldsay

Sheep and kirk,
croft and lighthouse,
wreck on treacherous reef;
green, gold, grey,
crumbling stone, lichen-
covered – every inch
could have been touched
by hand, hoof or gull's
stick leg. Dig and dig,
find new meaning in
layers of soil, of
genealogy.
Re-invent
this subtle, parallel
place, that makes north
true, possible, outlined,
like a ghost's drawn breath.

When you leave

(for Alex)

Walk on the cracks between the flagstones,
turn in through the blue gate,
touch the warm stone.
(Two hundred years ago, hands that shaped it
flinched at Napoleon's name.)

The garden, neglected,
explodes with summer beauty;
Brinkie's Brae is flowered and the Hoy hills,
rock strewn on sun-shot heather,
guard the town.

Cast loose like the ferry ropes
you'll leave as the year turns,
and Stromness receding from the Sound
will stay like an ancient image,
a first permanence.

Let twenty unassuming piers
sustain you like healing fingers,
lift you beyond hurt and harm;
let them hold you,
carry you home.

Pamela Beasant

Wish I had...

...A coat like a duvet
(but stylish), heated pants,
a paper bag with eye-holes,
jelly round my toes.

...Intravenous coffee,
a detector for levels of chocolate
running low (and a dispenser),
a delivery of wine and marmite toast at 10 pm.

Celaen Chapman

I was born in 1972 and brought up by my grandparents in their council house in Birmingham. My grandmother gave up her job as a hospital cleaner and taught me to read from a book of *Aesop's Fables*. My grandfather was a night shift proof-reader with the *Birmingham Post and Mail*. He taught me to read from books about cowboys and spies.

In 1990 I started studying for a combined degree in Sign Language and Women's Studies at Wolverhampton University. I fell in love with Scotland on my first visit in February 1991, through the window of a diesel Intercity 125, just as the train pulled through the moors, towards Beattock Summit and straight into a blizzard. And I fell in love with Glasgow before I got off the same train, looking out through evening sleet and onto its derelict cinemas, soft stone tenements and its big brown river. A few months later I abandoned my degree for Glasgow and moved here on a different train, with my bike, a rucksack, and nowhere to live.

Sixteen years later I'm still in love. In 2001 I graduated from the University of Strathclyde with a degree in Community Education, and I'm currently completing a Masters in Creative Writing at the University of Glasgow.

I feel lucky to be here, now, in 2008, surrounded by such a strong and diverse community of women writers, some in Scotland, some living in other places, some emerging and some (hopefully) waiting to be re-discovered.

Celaen Chapman

Excision/ As Long as I Can Stay Here

I should have worn a thong. I should have bought something from Agent Provocateur. Something in red silk with a bit of leather. Something entertaining. I think the anaesthetist would have been entertained. The red silk would have caught his eye and then he would have looked and tried not to but looked again and maybe he would have made a comment, and I could have said something. What would I have said? I would have said: I bought it especially for today. I bought it especially for you. What do you think? And I would have smiled at him like I was Marlene Dietrich. In *The Blue Angel*, when she's half-dressed, off-stage, looking straight into the black and white eyes of the university professor who's just beginning to fall in love with her. What he said was: I'm not going to lie; it won't feel like just a scratch, it *will* sting. It was nice of him, to not lie.

The surgeon promised that this would take twenty minutes. She didn't smile. After the first incision I began counting the seconds and they went like this: One. Two. Fuck, that's a bit sore. Fuck. Try to smile convincingly. Three. Start again. Christ. One. That feels like ... that feels like she is pulling things out of me that have been all nice and warm and coiled and curled on top of one another and what if she doesn't put them back in properly. What if she doesn't put them back in coiled and curled how they were. Fucking *ow* fucking sore that fucking anaesthetic is really slow. It helps, thinking about lingerie, it's better than trying to count the seconds. Something in yellow satin with frills and bows curling around the tops of my thighs. Okay. What else. Something in powder blue with tie sides. Powder blue would make a nice combination with the green we are all wearing. Powder blue and surgical green. Norwegian. Like I imagine it would be if I took the mail boat from Bergen to the Arctic Circle. From the sea, there would be little harbours and there would be powder blue and surgical green wooden houses. Herring Huts. All lined up in the Norwegian dawn.

The anaesthetist is looking at a machine on stilts. It will be telling him things about my heartbeat and blood pressure and I wonder if in a hundred years time it could tell him about my thoughts. Imagine that. Your anaesthetist watching your thoughts while you are thinking them. Right now he would be watching a picture of an old mail boat sailing into the calm water harbour of Svolvær, and just to his left he would be able to hear the sound of arctic terns fighting over a scooped-up sand eel. There would be a seal on a rock making the shape of a black crescent moon. He might not realise it's a seal until he notices its tail flipper flexing up towards the sky. It's moving because the seal is a bit nervous of the incoming boat.

The anaesthetist looks over at me. I frill my fingers at him and I can feel a current of panic in the nerves and muscles all the way from the back of my neck to the tips of my fingers. It's a struggle to just frill my fingers, to just leave it at that. And smile. Smile. Smile. He says, how are you doing? And I say Fine. Fine. Really. I'm really bloody fantastic. Really bloody. Which makes me laugh, a little bit, without opening my mouth, but it's still enough to make my chest go up and down, inconveniently for the surgeon. Airinairoutairinairout. I can feel my lungs flapping at her.

She looks at me and sighs. She puts her hands in the air as if I'm holding a standard issue service revolver with the safety catch off. When I was wee I wanted to go to New York and join the police. I bought a New York Police Department arm badge and sewed it to my school bag. I wanted to be the blonde one off *Cagney and Lacey*. She had a yellow sports car and drank whisky, and after she threatened people with her service revolver she would go back to the locker rooms at the 14th Precinct and kick the metal locker doors because really, she had been scared when she had to point a service revolver at someone. The surgeon looks a bit like Cagney and I can just see her hands. She's holding a scalpel. I'm sorry, I say. It tickles. I wish I could see her hands without the gloves.

She must have good quick slow delicate dexterous fine artful canny nimble beautiful exquisite meticulous gentle hands. I hope she does. I hope her hands can be all of those things. I hope they can be all of those things at once and all of those things separately when they need to be. The latex gloves are cream and bloody, they are very dramatic. Usually I see things like these gloves and I think, remember, that's just strawberry-flavoured candyfloss syrup. I went to the Swan Theatre in Stratford once with school and the best thing was a man who worked for *Casualty* on TV and he showed us how to make fake fractured legs, fake ruptured arteries and eyeballs, fake sword punctures, fake stitches and skin contusions.

And he said that the actors all really loved it when they had to act getting hurt because then they could lick the strawberry syrup off themselves. And then on the bus home afterwards I thought about all the actors licking each other on stage until it turned into a kind of orgy and they all forgot their lines and the plot and the audience was full of reviewers for the papers so it turned into a sensation the next day. Moral degradation. Sign of the times. And the worst of it was that the stalls and the gods were full of school children. Corrupted, they would have been. From seeing grown men licking strawberry syrup from each other's nipples and thighs.

I look up at the surgeon and I want to say to her: I could lick that clean for you if you like; I could suck it from your fingers. But I don't because I have to remind myself she can't see into my thoughts with the machine and she doesn't know about the strawberry syrup and the actors. But that makes me laugh again, and it's gone a bit further than I intended so it also makes me blush and I have to look away from her for a minute, at the big articulated flying saucer that's lighting me up. It's got six bulbs in chrome casings and I can see six little reflections as she starts working again. I don't think she noticed me blushing, I'm very red already. I can feel blood running down the skin covering the ribs on my left side and settling into a little pool just under my shoulder blade. It's warm. It could be water. It's nice, how warm it feels. It could be antiseptic. Or saline. And they have warmed it up for me so that it feels just nice.

Fuck that really is really fucking sore now. Ow, I say. Before I can stop myself. It's an instinctive reflex *Ow*. The anaesthetist looks at the surgeon who has put her hands in the air again. She says, I think we really need to do a general. I smile up at her, trying to make it a sweet smile. No, sorry, I'm fine, I say, don't worry. She frowns and the anaesthetist gets down from his white moulded plastic swivel-chair. It looks like something from a 1970s space film when he's not sitting on it. The surgeon says, it'll be much better, this is really difficult for you, and there's no need, it'll be much better.

I've got contact lenses in, I say. You can't. She is looking at me and I think she might ask the student to remove them. I blink and swivel my eyes in circles, the way my optician taught me, making sure that the lenses are stuck to my eyes as fast as the suction cups the men at the garage use for lifting car windscreens into place. Even if I could take the lenses out myself it would be like taking my glasses off before I go to sleep. Taking my glasses off before I jump off a huge enormous fucking cliff the height of the Old Man of Hoy.

I would so much rather be climbing the Old Man of Hoy. Wearing hundreds of safety ropes and a crash helmet. The clean air eddying around my knuckles which would be carefully curled around a fold of rock and there would be the sloshy sea below me and fulmars and kittiwakes and oystercatchers and a seal watching me from all the way down. Maybe the same seal, the one from Svolvær. I'm sorry, I say, I forgot to take them out. I read about this on the internet last night. You can't wear contact lenses for a general anaesthetic because your eyes roll up and the lenses might get stuck in the eye cavity, on the wrong side of your eye, and that would be a bit of a mess to sort out.

You also can't eat before a general anaesthetic. I ate three bananas, a potato waffle and a punnet of strawberries about two hours ago, that's the emergency backup, I know they won't risk giving me a general if I tell them what I've eaten. Not eating is more important than remembering to take your contact lenses out because something can go wrong that means you might choke. It's because when you're lying down and you're anaesthetised the food can gurgle up from your stomach and end up in your lungs. It's weird to think of your stomach being empty and your lungs being full of food.

She says, Okay. But next time you really should get a general. We don't usually do this. If I was having an operation I would have a general. I wouldn't think twice. I want to tell her I don't believe her but she sighs and says: Okay, it's going to take a bit longer because there are some complications. It's nothing to worry about, it's just that the lump – the fibroadenoma, I say, making sure she knows she is dealing with someone who knows exactly what is happening – yes, she says, the fibroadenoma is caught behind some ... some fibres – ducts, I say – yes, she says, and it's quite intrinsic so I'll have to be careful getting it out. Okay, I say. That's fine.

Is it painful? She says it shouldn't be.

Yes, I say. Yes, it's a bit nippy. She looks at the anaesthetist. Can you top up the local? The anaesthetist nods and disappears behind me and the surgeon lets the student mop the side of my ribs while they're waiting. The student's nice, she looks apologetic and she's very gentle.

I'm happier now she's said it's okay. I'm relieved. I don't want to be put to sleep. It's because when I was wee I had teeth taken out and they still used gas and I think I nearly died. I can remember what happened: I was seven and my grandad walked me to the dentist and he was really nice to me while we walked, but it was a bit like he was going to leave me in a forest without a trail of crumbs.

It was guilty nice. When we got there, the dentist and the nurse were too friendly and they kept looking at each other like they were trying to reassure themselves that they could do what they were about to do. I liked the nurse, she was wee, the same height as me, and I had just reached the age where I was starting to fall in love randomly and all the time. In the week before my dentist appointment I had fallen in love with: the lollipop lady (I saved up for weeks and bought her a bag of Foxes Glacier Mints), the woman behind the counter at the cinema (where I bought the Glacier Mints), Lola Marcel wearing a feather boa and locked in a room in the Micky Finn Salon in Brushwood Gulch (the film I saw at the cinema after buying the mints), and even with Huckleberry Finn being a girl and trying to thread a needle to prove it (the programme that was on TV when I got home from the cinema, with the mints for the lollipop lady).

The anaesthetist walks between my covered right side and the machine on stilts, checking it as he goes past, then walks around my feet, which I can't see, and stops on my left side. He doesn't say anything this time. Ow. Fucking fuck. Fucking ow. I don't say it this time either. I smile and wince and smile again and say, thank you. He's very quiet and he makes me think of the poem I did at school, the one about being put to sleep by a soft embalmer with careful fingers. Ode to an anaesthetist, it should have been called. But I think it was something about poppies. Opium might be better than whatever it is he's been using. I close my eyes and pinch the edges of the plastic sheet on both sides of me with my thumbs and forefingers. I try and pinch hard enough to make a puncture through the plastic, but my nails are too short. The surgeon is telling the student about her holiday. She is going to the Azores next week. Warm seas, she is saying, amazing seafood. It's okay, I say, I'm fine, you can just carry on. She says, are you sure, you don't want to wait a bit for the anaesthetic? No, I say. I'm fine.

If I'd seen her again afterwards I would have fallen in love with the dental nurse. She looked like the new *Doctor Who* assistant, the one who was clever and a journalist and a feminist and wanted to know everything and got really angry at the Doctor when he asked her to make him a cup of coffee, because it was patronising. I was in the chair, not too different from this, all wheels and articulated joints and plush plastic underneath me, I was probably trying to pinch through the material with my fingernails, and they came at me with a hissing mask and the nurse said, all you need to do is breathe, just breathe naturally.

The dentist pressed the mask over my mouth and nose and I was blinking at them and they said, that's right, that's good, go to sleep. But they were a bit confused because I kept looking at the nurse and blinking; I was blinking at her for much longer than I should have been. It was because I was holding my breath. I think that was the problem, that then, eventually, when my ears were filled up with the sound of heart valves and whooshing and what I could see through my eyes was turning into TV static, I took an enormous gulp of gas, like one of the people in the *Poseidon Adventure* who's swimming through a sea-filled corridor and then they get their trouser leg caught on something and they are there for ages, scrabbling in bubbles, until someone helps them and they get to the surface at the other end of the corridor and they come up and suck the air in so hard they splash and choke and make themselves sick. It was like that, except I came up being pulled backwards through the inside of a funnel made out of spinning stars and blackness. I was much more flesh and blood than I should have been. I could put my left hand on the skin under my T-shirt. I could kick and wave. I still had all my clothes on. I was wearing my favourite pair of jeans, the ones with a flash of lightning stitched into the back pockets. I could see my new navy-blue trainers with miles of space and darkness underneath them. I screamed and yelled and kicked and tried to swim. I was flailing without a dentist's chair in a black hole and there was even a white light in the distance pulling me towards it. It felt like a very bad thing. I tried to swim for hours, until I was exhausted, and until I came back up screaming with my hands out in front of me, and then I grabbed at the nurse's hand and told her to run and I punched the dentist in the balls. My grandad heard me and came in from the waiting room and he saw the nurse and the dentist standing by the chair sweating and looking frightened. I was standing in the corner of the room next to the closed curtain with blood dribbling out of my mouth and down my chin.

I'm not doing that again. I'm happier staying here with the anaesthetist and the surgeon and the student, I'm happier looking around the room with my contact lenses in and my stomach filled with bananas and waffles and strawberries. I want to tell the surgeon, in future, she can cut into anything, my lungs or heart or spleen or spine or knees or brain or eyes, anything, as long as I can stay here with her while she does it.

Okay, she says, that's it, there we are, that's great. She hands a steel kidney dish to the student, and she looks at it, smiling, and says, wow. Then looks at me, still smiling, and says, it's the size of a kiwi fruit.

I want to say something less flippant, but I can't help it, I say, lovely. I don't ask to see it. On the ward this morning the surgeon called it a breast mouse and I wonder if the piece of me in the kidney dish will look like a skinned mouse, something creamy and veiny. Though a mole might be better, something burrowed. I can smell cauterising; it's like the smell our cat makes when it singes its whiskers in a candle. Then there is stitching, I can feel it, but the feeling has lost its precision because the anaesthetic is beginning to work. Then the surgeon says: All done. We'll take biopsies from the tissue and let you know. Try not to worry. I nod and I say thank you and she carries on looking at me so I look back up at the flying saucer light and she says: there is a good chance you'll be okay. She says this benignly and this is how I want it to be. Benign. Like a good fairy inside me, in disguise, non-aggressive, non-invasive, something full of kindness, all the way to the core. Like a pearl found in the centre of an onion. A gift unwrapped from soft tissues and milk ducts. A present for the pathologists. They can have it. I could put a label on it.

With all my love. Best wishes. All good things to you, always. x x x.

Okay, I say. Thanks. I know. I'm sure it'll be fine. And she smiles for the first time and leaves.

Then I'm covered over decently by the green sheet and I'm pushed out through the swing doors feet first and it's nice to be able to see my feet again. I wiggle my toes at myself. Then the wheels stop and I'm back on the ward and you're sitting in the visitor's chair. You're waiting for me with your coat over your arm. You've been reading and you look at me over the rim of your glasses. Hi, you say, smiling, how was it? You're trying not to, but I can see your insides are crawling at the thought of how it was. It was okay, I say. It was fine. You look at me. Really, I say, it was fine, it'll be fine. It'll be okay.

Alison Craig

Like many writers, I have always written – journals, letters, little stories. As a child, I devoured books, reading, often deep into the night with a light – once, a candle! – under the bedcovers. At ten, I told my teacher I wanted to be an author, and wrote my first 'book'.

Life began in Birmingham, coming to Scotland in 1981. Despite the painful fracture inflicted by that move, I knew within weeks I would never go back. I studied English and History at Strathclyde University from 1981 to 1985. There I met Professor Douglas Gifford, an inspirational man who fired me with passion for Scotland's language and literature.

Distracted by work and youth's agitations, it was a long time before I started writing 'properly'. In 1997, a course for beginner writers, tutored by Janet Paisley, gave me confidence in my ability and helped me find my voice.

Good writing cuts to the truth and pulse of life. Poetry does this with such immediacy, and this makes it my first love. Also, it's an easy focus when writing time is snatched between family, work and domestic concerns. However, I also write fiction, articles, sports reports and book reviews.

I came to womanhood late, too. Early on, I was acutely aware of my mother's entrapment by the traditional demands of her sex. I told her, aged four, that boys had a much better deal. At fifteen, I thought breasts and periods were a complete bind. But recent years – particularly but not exclusively since the birth of my daughter – have brought friendships with women of honesty, intelligence, humour and strength. Periods and breasts seem less important these days.

I live in the Ayrshire hills, the sea just a short drive away, willing captive to the fierce love that is Scotland.

Alison Craig

Dream Waker

A cot on a winter's evening, a child
Turns and sighs, fingers feeling for flowers
In the dark. Her mother watches, love wild
As sea, soft as rain, constant as night's hours,
Watches the small tug of dreams like still air's
Magician twitching leaves. Stops her own breath
To hear the sweet fill of tiny lungs. Theirs,
Blood   flesh   pain. The prophecy of fierce birth.

Don't listen, though, to these small black words. Hush.
Watch the soul's scripture on her face, words proud,
Gentle as moths around light. Know the push
Of dreams as she picks her way among clouds.

And she wakes, sleeps again, wakes to spring, skies
Wide, and dreams make tomorrow in her eyes.

Yesterday's Man

You came back to rock my soul
one day of indecent summer in February.
Searching the loft for a different history,
breathing sun-bathed wood, spinning dust
and something odd and sweet,
like cinnamon, or nostalgia.

In a darkening corner long forgotten,
veiled in plastic and a decade of stour,
a box. There, on top, gloves. Brown leather,
wool-lined. I remember the utter comfort.
Lift them now, so cool, take you to me again,
bury my face in you.

Time melts in my hands, drips through my fingers.
Knuckles stretched to bone-shine,
tendons stitched fiercely into the backs,
like love. Then place them together,
as if to drink you from their bowl.
Hollow fingers fall becalmed,
palms crease like desire, cupping memory,
catching breath-warmed days
and star-cooled, tangled midnights.

Your last letter said you don't recognise
the leaning sadness that is you, yesterday's man,
in the mirror. I pull on the gloves,
tug at their beating wrists, stretch fingers.
Feel their hot grip reaching into the soft of me.

Alison Flett

I was born and brought up in Edinburgh, which I still think of as my home, although I have been living in Orkney for the past eight years. I love island life, the constant presence of the sea and sky and the familiarity of faces, though sometimes I hanker after the noise and bustle and anonymity of the city.

When I lived in Edinburgh I mostly wrote poetry which was very urban-influenced, full of gritty realism and social comment; but living in Orkney, amongst other things, has changed both the focus and subject matter of my writing. In the last two or three years I've been bitten by the novel bug. I've just finished my first novel, set on a small (fictional!) island, and have now moved on to the second one. I had to start it towards the end of the first one, as I couldn't bear the thought of not having something to work on. Novel writing is so different from poetry, and I love how all-encompassing it is, the constant cross-referencing of novel and real life. I can't imagine living without it now!

When Sharon asked me for a piece for this anthology I didn't think I would be able to come up with anything, as I was so engrossed in the novel. However, I met the wonderful writer and storyteller Janet McInnes at a writers' retreat where we were both running workshops. I ended up going to her workshop, and this is the story that came out of it…

Alison Flett

Two Sides

SARAH'S SIDE

Ah'd telt him tae clear off but he wiz still standin there, ah could hear him, the pat-pat of his bare feet on the concrete. He thought if he jist stood there long enough ah wiz gonnae let him back in. Aye, that *would* be right!

Ah hear ye Shug! ah said. Ah ken ye're still oot there. Ye're no gettin in, but.

Ach c'moan doll, says Shug. Have a heart wid ye? It's bloody freezin oot here.

Away an bile yir heid, ah says. That'll warm ye up.

There wiz the creak o the letterbox flap oan his sidey the door liftin up, an he started whisperin through it. Sarah ... he wiz goin. Sarah...

Ah hunkered doon so's ah could hear his words better but ah didnae lift the flap oan ma sidey the door. Ah didnae lift the flap an ah didnae see his big broon eyes, pleadin at me through the gap in the door between us.

See us some clothes oot here at least doll, Shug says. Thinky Mrs McPherson next door. Christ if she comes oot intae the stair the now an sees me standin here in the buff, she'll likely have a heart attack... Sarah... Are ye listenin...? Ye're pittin her life at risk, Sarah.

Ah didnae say anythin. Ah wiz done speakin. Time wiz, we'd sit for hours, the two of us. Bletherin, bletherin, bletherin. Lyin in oor bed sometimes, makin love, bletherin, laughin, makin love again. Aye, time wiz, right enough. No any mare but.

The letterbox flap banged doon an he started thumpin oan the door. Sarah, he said. Open up. Right now... Sarah! he shouted. Open up!

Ah shuffled ma bum across the carpet, away fae the door, an sat against the opposite waw. Ah could see the door jump an shiver wi each fist-thump. Sarah! he wiz shoutin. Sarah!

Ah met Shug in a café. We were both oan a lunch break an there wisnae many seats left so he asked if he could sit at my table. Ah said aye. Too right he could! Ah fancied him straight off tae tell the truth. We got talkin an he had this crazy big smile an a kindy deep throaty laugh. We ended up the both of us skivin off work that afternoon. We were in bed afore tea-time.

Ah thought we were in love, maybe we were, but if we were where did it go? The way he touched me, the way we looked at each other, the things we talked aboot, the things that made us laugh. Standin side by side tae brush oor teeth at the sink, his shoes beside mine at the door. It wisnae that long ago either, hardly mare than a year, an look at us now, look what we're daein tae each other.

Ah've kent aboot the other lass for a good while now, but it must've been goin oan a long time afore ah realised. Ah found the lass's texts one day when he forgot his phone. Needless tae say, ah checked the outbox too, an ah found all Shug's texts back. Ah didnae say anything but, jist put the phone back where it wiz. Ah've waited, see, ah've bided ma time.

He's ayeways been a sleepwalker, at least twice a week, specially if he's a drink in him. It's no the first time he's gone right oot the hoose either. Ah woke up as he wiz gettin oot the bed an ah waited tae see where he went. Soon as ah heard the front door, that was me, up and oot the bed like a shot. Ah hud the door banged shut an the sneck on, quick as a flash, then ah keeked through the spy-hole tae see him. The bang must've woke him cause he wiz skyin aboot wi that glaikit look he has when he first comes roond. The look changed tae panic when he realised where he wiz, an totally in the noddy an all. He put his hands doon tae try an cover his bits and he hurried over tae the door. He started ringin the bell like a daftie. Ah shouted through the door that he could stop the ringin, ah wiz right there, an he wisnae gettin in. Ah telt him what ah kent, an ah said ah'd hud it up tae there. Ah said he could clear off tae the other lassy's hoose.

The thumpin's stopped noo, he's gave up that game at least. Probably worried aboot noisin up the neighbours. Ah crawl across the floor and sit by the door again, ma lug pressed against it, to see if ah can hear him. Nothing. Ah stand up an have a wee spy through the hole but there's nae sign of him oot there. I feel sick thinkin maybe he *has* gone tae the other lassy's. I turn away and lean with ma back against the door, then ah slide doon it till ah'm sittin oan the carpet. Ah sit there an ah start tae greet, don't ask me why.

Sarah? It's his voice, right close oan the other sidey the door. He must be crouched doon behind it, like me. Sarah, are you OK? he's sayin. Ah stop greetin. Ah wipe ma nose oan ma tee-shirt. Ah still dinnae say anythin but. I love you Sarah, he says, an ah believe he means it, ah jist dinnae ken whit he means by love.

SHUG'S SIDE

When I came to I was bare naked and standing outside in the cold. Fuck, I thought. Fucking hell. What if one of the neighbours comes out their door, sees me standing in the stair in the buff. I could see the door had shut behind me but, thank christ, Sarah was inside. I rang the bell. Riiiiing. Riiiiiiiiing. That's when I realised Sarah was already there. She shouted at me through the door.

I ken all about it Shuggy, she said. There's no point pretending any more.

I panicked then, I can tell you. I thought, shit! What's she found out? My head started pounding and I felt sick.

Ken all about what, doll? I shouted back. I don't ken what you're on about.

You and that Tina lassy, she said. And don't bother acting the innocent.

Look, I don't ken who's been saying what, doll, I said, but it's a pack of lies, honest to god. Let us in Sarah, ay? Come on, ay? Let us in and we'll talk about it properly.

Ha! she said, nobody's said nothing, you stupid arse. I found her messages on your phone.

Fuck, fuck, fuck, I thought. Fucking fuckitty fuck. I really thought I might throw up. Sarah, doll, I said, we can't talk about this through a door. Let us in so we can sort it out.

I'm not wanting to sort it out, she said. I've had it up to here. You can fuck off to her house and sort it out.

Oh jesus, I thought, she's serious about this. She's really not going to let me back in. I was totally shiting it then, I really didn't ken what to do. All I kent was I'd made a big mistake. I mean Tina, man, fuck! Total sex on legs. Even the way she walks is sexy. But Sarah. Sarah's the one I love. She's the one I want to be with. And it wasn't like I hadn't thought about it before, but it was a bit like it suddenly hit me. I mean, what the fuck was I playing at, really, what the fuck was going on in my head?

When I was wee I mind listening to my folks arguing, all those arguments through the bedroom wall. My dad carrying on with this woman or that, and I always thought, how could he? If he loves my ma, how could he? My mate Chris says there's no such thing as love, he says it's all just biological reactions. He says it's chemicals that get released into your brain when you see something you associate with sex. And when you really really fancy someone, there's that many chemicals firing into your brain that you imagine it's something bigger, you think it's love.

It was that bloody nippy I started running on the spot, trying to warm myself up a bit. Sarah shouted again through the door, told me I still wasn't getting in. I thought, well, at least she's still there, that's a good sign. Maybe she'll listen to me now. I bent down and tried speaking to her through the letterbox, appealing to her better nature. She didn't answer but, so then I got angry and I started banging on the door. Sarah! I went. Sarah! Open up!

After a while I stopped. It wasn't getting me anywhere. It was all quiet on the other side of the door, I didn't even ken if she was still there. I felt really weak, like my legs weren't strong enough to hold me up any more, and I sank down onto the cold concrete floor. I leant back against the door, hugging my bare knees with my bare arms. For some reason I started thinking about the old couple on the train. It had happened ages ago, when I was on this train going south, there was an old couple sitting at the table across the aisle from me. They were all ancient and wrinkly looking and they weren't saying much, they were just sitting there holding hands. Folk were getting on and off, some of them sat down at the old couple's table. They'd get up again a few stops down the line and maybe someone else would get on and sit down at the table. The old folk just smiled at all the different people, still holding onto each other's hand. They held hands for the whole of their journey. They had to let go when it came to their stop, though. The man got up first and he waited while the wifie got up, and he helped her down the aisle, one hand under her elbow. I looked out the window as the train whizzed off and I seen them tottering across the platform together.

There's a noise at the other side of the door and I realise Sarah's still there. It sounds like she might be greeting. Sarah? I go. Sarah, are you OK? She doesn't answer but I can hear her sniffing and all I want to do is hold her hand. I love you, Sarah, I say, and I mean it. I really believe that what I'm feeling is love.

Jackie Kay

Jackie Kay was born and brought up in Scotland. She has published five collections of poetry for adults – *The Adoption Papers* (winner of a Forward Prize, a Saltire Award and a Scottish Arts Council Book Award), *Other Lovers* (which won the Somerset Maugham Award), *Off Colour* (shortlisted for the 1999 TS Eliot Award), and *Life Mask* and *Darling* (both Poetry Book Society Recommendations.)

Her first novel, *Trumpet* (Picador, 1998) won the Guardian Fiction Prize, a Scottish Arts Council Book Award and The Author's Club First Novel Award. It was also on the shortlist for the IMPAC award.

Her new collection of short stories, *Wish I Was Here* won the Decibel Writer of the Year award.

Jackie is a fellow of The Royal Society of Literature and is Professor of Creative Writing at Newcastle University. Her new collection of poetry for children, *Red, Cherry Red* has just been published by Bloomsbury. She lives in Manchester with her son.

Jackie Kay

Highland Girl

We were friends before we ever met, Highland girl –
On a holiday back then, I twirled
Round – there you were, Avielochan, aged eleven.
Later, your reflection in a window in Inverness.
You, sleeping, in the top bunk bed in Torridon.
You, dreaming on that bus going round Loch Ness.
It was you in that photo standing by the old Morris,
Aged two, farmyard, Wester Ross, next to the collie.
You were the girl waving as we left for Applecross.
When we caught the ferry from Oban to Tobermoray,
You fed the gulls with me on that dappled crossing.
We didn't go, though, to Aviemore, or ski on the Cairngorms.

We suddenly turned up on the isle of Mull,
Sitting on the roof of the old croft, talking
And talking till the moon slid down the corrugated iron.
We built a castle, jewelled with fragile shells
On the fine white sands of Calgary Bay.
You never made it to Dornoch in '73,
But to the south of Skye. Nor to Thurso
Tongue, or John O'Groats. You hung around Lossiemouth,
Beauly and Nairn, near where you came from,
Near where I nearly came from, where an Aunty now lives
Who collects spoons from all over the world,
Who has never been to Plockton or to Skye.

You were the bird; I was the wing. Bonny boat.
Once, on the Road to the Isles, we met; our parents
Sang *Westering Home*, drinking drams at Drumnadrochit.
We stayed up late with our listening faces,
Then stood for an age, another time, staring
At The Northern Lights of old Aberdeen,
Then, dear one, we made up our mind,
The blue of your eye, the brown of mine,
To be lifelong friends. So that when we met,
Our friend past was already known
To the places we had been and seen,
And each of those places nodded a polite Highland assent
Or danced a fierce Highland fling.

Sylvia Hays

I am a painter, despite having been forbidden to go to art college (it *had* to be university, universities; degrees in German and, at last, art). After a period as an academic nomad I came from the US to live in England (Oxford) in the '70s, but yearned for Scotland.

In the '80s I discovered Orkney for myself, on my bicycle, drawn there by 1) George Mackay Brown's poetry; 2) the St. Magnus Festival; 3) its rich archaeology. By then I was using archaeology as a metaphor for what I was doing in painting: trying to understand the land, trying to get below the surface of appearances, even trying to reach a broader (collective) unconscious response.

By the time the '90s came around I was splitting my life between Edinburgh and Orkney. In 2002 I found a site in Orkney for the house and studio I'd always wanted, and now live and work here permanently.

Orkney, both land and people, has always given me a sense of homecoming. I've found freedoms which I cherish: freedom to wander about anywhere in light or darkness; freedom from pigeon-holing or being pigeon-holed. So many people here have at least two occupations: fisherman and farmer, accountant and musician, dentist and artist. And so it is with me: I am almost new to writing, but not quite. As a closet poet, I wrote a little thirty years ago and a little more about ten years ago. Recently writing has become more important and indeed necessary to me. I intend to keep juggling both occupations.

Sylvia Hays

Night Walk

The other day she came across this:

> '22 November 1991 (walking home from Violet's house, 4.45 pm onwards)
>
> In the dark and watery land a torn cloud allowed a measure of light to pass, briefly, on its way to an early horizon. Light revealed water: water lying on the land where last month cattle stood, water in a lustrous film along the newly-paved track which pointed the way to the lighthouse before being absorbed by darkness. The Firth needed no light, though its edge was marked by an amber chain of lights on the mainland and its length was probed by beacons. Sound was the dark's essence. The tide swept in beneath the cliffs, sucking and spewing in the caves and geos and contradicting the rush of waters ebbing from rocks and skerries. Stop. Look back at the small square lighted windows of Violet's house with tea, cat, stove, and a row of crocheted dolls inside. Look past the blue flickering rectangle of cartoon shows in the caravan, look towards home, below in darkness between the vanished track and the lighthouse. Turn around and look north where on a summer midnight banks of cloud will hover just above the sun and turn to flame. Walk on beside the ditch where water churns and gasps from recent rain. Try not to use the torch to see the track. It is black now, but the ditch is blacker. Try to…'

Try to what? After so many years she couldn't remember what would have come next. The cheap Woolworth's notebook paper was rust-marked and crimped with damp. In the margin with a different ink she had written 'water'. Below it 'eventually another section: "wind", etc.' Trying to connect herself with the elements, presumably. Trying to place herself. One night when she had lain at the crossroads on her back and become a crucifix or a compass her head had pointed north to the possibility of the aurora borealis; on her left hand was the neolithic Tomb of the Eagles; on her right the approach to Scapa Flow. Home was at her feet in a direct line to the lighthouse in the Pentland Firth. She had called it home years before and felt it still, though it was hardly more than an encampment, meant to be temporary. Before that year she had written nothing and since then nothing; her other occupations and critical senses acted as brakes. She was embarrassed by poetic effusions, however private, and confounded by the power of the word to falsify as it is written. How to write 'I' without the *I* intruding. Why write at all? Was living a life not enough? What if it *was* an unwritten life? To stake a claim on existence it seemed necessary to transform. The physical had to become the metaphysical. Mental events had to become physical events, otherwise they would go out of existence when the brain died. She had lain in the road and become the points of the compass; she had lain on the lichen-covered angled rocks which formed an arena in front of the Tomb above the cliffs and imagined herself excarnated on twiggy scaffolding, her bones being picked clean by sea eagles, but if no-one knew this did it make any difference? Perhaps she needed to posit a camera in the sky, somewhere high above the meeting of the Atlantic and the North Sea, to connect her small life here with the rest of the world. The camera would be not so much an instrument of paranoia as one of philosophical idealism: a contemporary version of Bishop Berkeley's mind of God whose omniscience was all that prevented things from going out of existence if no-one happened to be thinking of them. And then, in the same damp notebook, she had copied out this:

> 'You know, you are born in a place and you grow up there. You get to know the trees and the plants. You will never know any other trees and plants like that… Here you wait for the poui to flower one week in the year and you don't even know you are waiting. All right, you go away. But you will come back. Where you born, man, you born.'
> V.S. Naipaul: *The Mimic Men*

She wasn't born in Mississippi. But her parents were. Ancestors had straggled down from Virginia where their own ancestors had first landed. They laid claim to the land, as they had in Virginia, were pioneers at first and eventually became Old Families. 'Home' to her parents, especially to her mother, always meant Mississippi. But in that place she was an alien and wished to remain so, despite the rich seams of memories that invaded her from time to time. Her mother began in Mississippi and ended there, in the red clay dust. In between there was Long Island, there was Virginia, getting nearer the mother's home.

Imprisoned by temperament and later by alimony, occasionally her mother would say, 'I've got cabin fever. Let's go somewhere.' And they would go, with her little sister in the back seat of the green Buick, vomiting. Sometimes they would end up in Pennsylvania Dutch country, looking for barns with painted hex signs that her mother would note down or pottering in antique and craft shops, an occupation unendurable to the girls. Once they headed west, even in the 1950s not an easy thing to do. The Appalachians had been settled from the north, by people filtering down the valleys, rather than from the early settlements to the east. Later on, stagecoach routes threaded through the few mountain gaps. Even when the railways came they stopped at the slopes of the Blue Ridge and handed their passengers on to the stagecoach. Finally the Frenchman Claudius Crozet engineered the completion of the railway through one gap across the mountains but not before a hundred Italian labourers died in an epidemic of smallpox.

The mother with her two girls followed the same route west across the Blue Ridge into the Shenandoah Valley and slowly snaked across the ribs of the Alleghenies. In the coal mining country of West Virginia the two-lane road followed the railway line and the river; there was no other way. They drove slowly behind coal trucks through heavy grey air that blotted out the sun and destroyed lungs. Pools of dull water lay everywhere; streams were opaque and colourless. Unpainted, hip-roofed houses built of wood were propped on precipitous slopes. They were built into the mountainside at the back but were four or five stories at the front where the ground fell away. Galleried porches on every floor were supported by wooden stilts. How many families might have shared them they didn't know. The washing lines strung between the porch posts held laundry on which grey had laid a permanent claim. At one house they noticed a row of geraniums, bright red, someone's brave attempt. At another there was a thin girl of about six with a pale hopeful face and stringy hair. Islets of prosperity lay in wooded hills with little hand-painted signs advertising craft shops. Always there followed descents into narrow mining valleys where rail, road and river ran in a three-stranded ribbon.

Years later the mother was in an intensive care bed, dying. The daughter had never seen anyone dying before. The woman had become middle-aged since they had last met. She lay on her back under a white sheet whose thinness revealed the contours of her body and involuntarily the younger woman thought of the time when her mother must have lain thus after giving her birth. Parts of the body were dead already. Her fine and elegant hands were stiff and blue. Her feet, hidden by the sheet, were certainly without life. Across her face was beginning to spread a fine network of small blue veins. An hour later they had grown into a map as clearly defined as the maps of the daughter's childhood.

Maps were memorized against the day when she would run away from home, travelling the twelve hundred miles by bicycle to Mississippi. She had fixed the route in her mind on every journey back to grandparents. She rehearsed how she would camp, just off the road in the woods. For good measure she would take some schoolbooks with her so she might be taken for just any local child on her way to school. She had an ally in one or two aged relatives in Mississippi. Or so she thought.

One winter her hands held an aeronautical map to navigate the little Stinson her father flew, but she got them lost in a snowstorm. Her mittens were lost, her hands were freezing, but at eight years old she was too proud to cry. Then they recognized the tip of the Empire State Building poking through the whiteness. They picked up the radio beacon, correlated it with the one on the map and followed it back to the airstrip on Long Island.

In the cold of her new island home it should have been easier to think of her mittenless hands numbly clutching the aeronautical map a few thousand feet above New York but somehow Mississippi intruded again. From this northern treeless latitude she thought of that baking hill country, its red soil depleted by generations of cotton and tobacco. Eventually the farmers had been persuaded to replant with trees and the hills were cloaked with pine: short-leaf, long-leaf, loblolly, their scabby bark smelling of turpentine and their needles a listless green.

Here she didn't need trees. They would have been wrong in this open land, scoured by the Ice Age and scoured again by wind. The succession of land and sea and sky was so vast that objects here took on a significance they would never have had in conditions of urban clutter or topographical complication. The neolithic tomb on its clifftop eyrie, the sunk or grounded hulks that told of war or shipwreck, the rusty deep freeze washed up beside the Firth – all were markers which achieved the status of monuments simply by their presence. She could place herself here.

Caesarian

In that time when life was
circumscribed by tractors
I slid through spring mud,
climbed the midden ramp
into earth-hued byres.

The vet, a hard man (self-styled)
from Fair Isle, caught a whiff of
town or south about me, said
'If you faint deed away there's
no-one going to pick you up,'
and placed the tray of instruments
into my hands. I became not
a witness but an acolyte.

The heifer stood quietly at anchor
as the anaesthetic took hold.
The first incision drew
a red line on a brown flank,
and a second and a third,
unlayering the calf.

Tall and strong-armed Stephen
stepped out of shadows
found the Charollais hoof-points
and, hoisting arms overhead,
hauled the animal into life.

Sylvia Hays

There was a moment's Caravaggio,
all slanting light, deep penumbra, a
glistening diagonal taking breath,
then hasty deposition into straw.

I stood mindful of my station.
The tray offered curved needle, string.
I heard instructions as to the sewing-up
of live beef, each stitch
sealed against unravelling.

Before the last layer was sewn
there came a rustling nuzzling,
the newborn's senses finding feet,
imprinting mother on his calf-brain,
while I, unmoving as a caryatid,
let him imprint on mine.

Erica Munro

I live in the Highlands; always have, apart from the six years of lawyer training that took me south. It's nice – my family's here and I'm happy. I hope I'd say the same if I came from Paisley, Portsmouth or Peru.

Being a Highlander means I get the best hills and beaches, the funniest people and an extraordinary history from which to learn. But I'm defined by my human relationships and my choices, not by my beautiful domicile and its baggage.

I write contemporary fiction under my own name and collaborate with a funky London company writing women's fiction, using interesting pseudonyms. It's the closest I ever come to being mysterious.

Obstinately, I escape to write in a little flat in Central London whenever I can, in order to get some peace and quiet from the hurly-burly of my Black Isle life. But most of the time I'm a Highland GP's wife and a mother of three, who writes.

Erica Munro

'What Kept You?'

THE RUNE OF HOSPITALITY
I saw a stranger yestreen;
I put food in the eating place,
Drink in the drinking place,
Music in the listening place;
And, in the sacred name of the Triune (God),
He blessed himself and my house,
My cattle and my dear ones.
And the lark said in her song,
Often, often, often,
Goes the Christ in the stranger's guise;
Often, often, often,
Goes the Christ in the stranger's guise.
(Old Gaelic Rune recovered by Kenneth McLeod)

It hadn't gone as well as Isla had hoped. Three hours she'd stood, smiling until her cheeks ached, all open postures and approachability. Her purple silk mini-dress had orange-edged Maid Marian sleeves and her thick green tights wrinkled a little over embroidered shoes. She'd come as a flower, fresh and full of hope. Around her, the pale shades of indifference on the faces of the thin crowd were like negatives to the flamboyance of her paintings on the walls.

It was to be a homecoming, a celebration of the achievements of sons and daughters of the island who had gone away to live their lives in other places, yet whose work reached back to where they came from in so many diverse ways that holding a festival to draw them all back again had seemed to be an idea not only of breathtaking simplicity, but also of audacious innovation.

Thus was Isla tempted, along with the folk singer, the violinist, the actor, the Strathclyde Police Chief, the fashion designer, the writer of dirty stories, the felt-maker, the Commonwealth Games shot-putter, the cyber-animator, the pilot, the poet, the thrash metal band and the Gaelic weather girl, to tiptoe home, her best work bunched in the boot of her car, and take part in a gathering of returned natives, christened, with irresistible whimsy: *What Kept You?*

Her mother, still marooned, warned her that the organisers had been kicking up a bit about the event. The Chairperson was on record in the local paper as saying that the organisational logistics had been time-consuming and complicated, but that he and his committee were working hard to have workable solutions in place in time for the opening.

Funding, too, had raised hackles. Money allocated from this budget or that budget was either late, lower than promised, withdrawn entirely or never there at all until finally, the week before the opening, the paper couldn't even mention the festival without bolting on the prefix: *'Crisis-hit'*.

Isla slipped unnoticed into her own opening night. Her paintings looked different on the scuffed white wall; out of order, their story chopped and mixed like a dismantled jigsaw. She wished she'd insisted on staying and supervising the hanging but this hadn't been encouraged – the organisers had a squad on – and she hadn't wanted to be difficult. The man on the committee to whom she had given her sweated-over handwritten list of titles had typed it up in alphabetical order, and the canvasses hung accordingly.

A surge of visitors arrived to view her work during the hour before the folk singer started up across the square, and then there was a lull, followed by a slow trickle that moved between her exhibition and the felt-maker's display out in the annexe. She stood close to the drinks table, hanging on to her glass and her smile, saying 'thank you for coming' to the islanders. And to her mother, who took everything in with a single glance around the room, and gave her a wink.

She had never held with the notion that people were different on the island from how they were in the city. Tonight's mix was similar to any visitor to any exhibition in any city or town – a little older, perhaps, but the thick, hold-your-breath silences, the shuffling of feet, the murmurings and the throat-clearings were all the same. She said to the man who'd remarked that anyone could knock out this sort of stuff that she often heard that. And funnier.

Twenty years ago she'd danced in this hall. Pas-de-basques and high cuts, being shouted at by Miss Mackinnon, going over on her fat little ankles, stopping for interval crisps. That was Tuesdays. Thursdays she was a Brownie here, later a Guide. Round the back was where she'd had her first kisses at youth club discos, dismayed that boys liked to poke their tongues in girls' mouths.

Isla didn't know many of the people who came to the exhibition, but that wasn't a surprise – the island wasn't *that* small. And eleven years was a long time to be away. The changes, she saw, had been more than surface-deep; the whole place had been ploughed and replanted in the past decade, a tender rotation of natural selection, necessity and dreams.

Around her two committee members filled and refilled glasses until tipping point was reached and it was time for the Chairperson to make a speech. He spoke about how the exhibition had come together, whose idea it was, who was the powerhouse behind the organisation and what wouldn't have been possible without the co-operation of whom. He talked of the likelihood of *What Kept You?* becoming an annual event, and applause tickled the walls. He quipped about running out of talent to bring back, but that wouldn't matter, there was plenty still *in situ*. Then, no doubt realising he'd just shot a hole through his concept, he steadied, and asked everyone to raise their glasses to the future of the event.

At half-past ten the last visitor had gone home and Isla was poked down the road to the Chairperson's house for some late hospitality. The folk singer and the felt-maker went with her.

A hospitality sub-committee had been put in place to deliver food and beverages to the performers. The Chairperson's wife welcomed everyone warmly before showing them through to her kitchen, where a table was set for dinner. Artist, felt-maker and folk singer sat awkwardly, each upon a mis-matched chair, around a shoogly refectory table. The folk singer squeezed into the corner, scarlet beneath his grey beard, and the felt-maker's offer of help with the food was refused.

They talked amongst themselves, surrounded by the backs of the helpers, who jostled to pull trays of food out of the oven and lay them on the table for the performers to eat.

Isla remembered this house when it was the manse. The minister and his wife brought up five children here, one of whom had been her contemporary in school – his had been the first tongue poked in her mouth, come to think of it.

The food was nice and the felt-maker, a vegetarian, was offered onion quiche. They talked of their lives away from the island, groping for common ground in between mumbled thanks as more dishes of food were put in front of them. The helpers were biblically busy, worrying over how much more to prepare, who else might arrive.

Isla wished the eating was over so that she could go home; it was awkward, receiving hospitality from all those backs.

One was washing dishes as though in a race, two clambered over each other to dry and stack. Another had to leave, saying she'd be back the following night at seven, and not a *moment* before – the others had laughed at that.

At last Isla, the felt-maker and the folk singer rose from the table and thanked the hostess for the hospitality. The folk singer said he couldn't remember ever going to a festival that had such hospitality. The felt-maker said now she remembered what Highland hospitality was all about. Isla, saying nothing, drove home, her gifts for her mother beside her in the car.

Gerda Stevenson

I was born and brought up in the village of West Linton, in the Scottish Borders, and have returned to live just two miles down the road from my birth place. I'm a homing pigeon, and love the Pentland Hills – 'The Hills of Home,' as Robert Louis Stevenson called them. I became aware of literature at a very early age, partly because my father, the composer/pianist Ronald Stevenson, has always worked closely with words, setting many poetic texts to music, including work by Hugh MacDiarmid, William Soutar and Sorley MacLean. I've been acting and writing since childhood, and for over thirty years I've worked professionally as an actor/director/writer, in theatre, radio, opera, film and television throughout Britain and abroad. My poems have appeared in *The Scotsman, Cencrastus, The Eildon Tree,* and *Parnassus* (the New York poetry magazine). My pamphlet, *Invisible Particles,* was published in 2002. I was runner-up in the Eildon Tree *Wilderness* poetry competition, 2005, and published in the subsequent anthology. I've written extensively for radio, dramatising the novels of neglected Scottish women writers Mary Brunton and Nancy Brysson Morrison, and, most recently, Sir Walter Scott's epic *The Heart of Midlothian.*

I'm keenly aware of the importance of ensuring that women's voices are heard, which is why I founded *Stellar Quines*, now Scotland's leading women's theatre company (and with which I commissioned and directed Janet Paisley's brilliant award-winning play *Refuge*, a portion of which is – finally – published in this anthology). I'm Associate Director of *Communicado*, and there's nothing I love more than the collaborative nature of theatre – getting into a rehearsal room with a group of actors to create the world of a play. As a member of the Pentlands Writers' Group, I co-wrote, edited and directed a large-scale community play, *Pentlands at War,* based on local memories, recently published by Scottish Borders Council. I regularly work at Oran Mor in Glasgow, where I've directed plays by Jackie Kay, Anne Donovan, Catherine Czerkawska and Peter Arnott. I have a strong feeling of being part of an artistic community in Scotland, something I value hugely – I only wish the government would understand the importance of the arts as a foundation stone of any civilised society.

www.gerdastevenson.co.uk

Gerda Stevenson

Co-op Funeral Parlour

My heart stops
at the waxed apple cheeks, plump
and impossibly polished;
your head in my palm yesterday,
skull barely masked by paper skin,
you were undeniably mine.
An imposter lies in this small white box
we ordered – a collector's doll,
lace-framed face mounted
on a slice of shop-window silk.
I would strip the pinned folds, find
the miracle of your miniature hands,
blood cooled to blue beneath each nail,
but a tail of brown thread,
carelessly trimmed, curls
below the jaw's angle, a worm
emerging from puckered skin.
I draw back, let panic drain,
search for signs of you,
and detect at last
the down-turn of your top lip –
my mouth's copy –
under a lipstick blur.

First Love

'Let's walk,' he said, 'down that line of trees,'
so they left the road, and the field swayed
its seed-laden skirt, blood on the hem
from a low-spilling sun,
no words while they walked,
but a pleating of fingers,
the clamour of ravens' call in their ears.

'Take the bus,' he said, 'to my student room,'
so in after-school dusk, she left the wind-scoured
hills of home, and pressed a hot cheek
to the shuddering glass, cool balm
through the long miles in December's gloom.

Rasp of gear-change, wheeze of brakes,
and she steps at last into Edinburgh's shroud;
kirk spires dissolve, looming street-lamps
lead her on (virgin footsteps voiceless now
in the veiled air) and there's no going back,
past the college gate he enters each day,
down a cobbled lane to the winding well
of the tenement stair,
the cauldron she climbs
to his door.

'A cold night for it!'
the landlady croons,
casting her judgement
from the banister above,
linoleum glare and Calvin's zeal
glistening in a covert glance.

Moonlight and sleet on the windowsill;
the clock-tower tolls its tale of the last bus,
long gone, long gone.
Hand in hand they chime their challenge
into the stairwell, carol each landing
down to the street, Holly and Ivy,
Feast of Stephen, Lo! A Star,
and foot it back, home to the hills
in the frosted air.

Agnes Owens

Agnes Owens was born in 1926 in the village of Milngavie near Glasgow, where poverty was the order of the day and most people were on the dole. Her mother told her of snatching a three-penny bit off the mantelpiece in case the means-test man saw money lying about. After ten years on the dole her father got a job in the local paper mill, which allowed them to go holidays 'doon the water'. He died aged forty-seven years of wounds sustained in the First World War, which was a great blow to Agnes and her young brother. Her mother married again when Agnes had obtained an office job as filing clerk in a firm where she met her future husband. Perhaps due to being at Anzio in the Second World War, he died at forty-three, leaving her to bring up four children. She married again, had three more children, and lives to this day with her present husband: all of which led to her joining a writing class "just to have a night out away from the house". Her first attempt at writing was a short story about a fat filthy woman called Arabella. In 1984, her story collection *Gentlemen of the West* was published and received the Scottish Arts Council Autumn book award. Then came the novels *Like Birds in the Wilderness* (1987) and *A Working Mother* (1994), the story collection *People Like That* (1996), and the novel *For the Love of Willie* (1998) for which she received Scottish Writer of the Year award. *Lean Tales* (1985) was a story collection shared with Alasdair Gray and Jim Kelman. Her novellas *Bad Attitudes* and *Jen's Party* were published in 2003, and led to all her short stories being published, along with fourteen new ones, in *Agnes Owens: The Complete Short Stories* (2008).

Agnes Owens

Oh Brother

Standing there under the mid-day sun and hearing the minister go on and on about love that transcends death I could not help wondering if my parents had ever loved me. I could not remember many signs of it. Perhaps I had been an unlovable child. Yet I remember Dad taking me to the bowling green when I was five years old and he reigned there as champion. I would run on to the green shouting, 'Throw it in the ditch, Dad!' under the illusion that men were trying to do that with the bowls. Afterwards he would lift me up in the air by my hands and twirl me round till I was nearly sick, calling me his little princess. That was before my baby brother arrived.

My mother obviously loved *him*. She watched over him, oohing and aahing, then told me to change his nappy as she couldn't stand the smell. At that time Dad was always out working or at the bowling green, the pub or the football and I was no longer his little princess. To make matters worse I had to hurl George in his pram up and down the pavement while my mother got on with the shopping or the washing. When I gave him his breakfast he usually spat baby porridge out over my jumper. If I nipped his leg in retaliation he screamed loud enough to burst a gut. No wonder I wanted to kill him. The opportunity arose when my mother asked me to take him to the swimming baths. She said, 'He's almost three years old and it's time he learned to swim.'

My plan was to hold him under water in the paddling pool, but it misfired. I lost my balance and fell in. George saved my life, shrieking like a dervish until an attendant came and pulled me out.

'It was all your fault!' I told George. 'If you hadn't been hanging on to me I wouldn't have fell in.'

He believed me and said, 'Don't tell Mummy, she'll hit me.'

This was a lie. It was only me she hit. I said, 'Well, keep your mouth shut and I won't tell.'

Of course George couldn't help telling. He was coming up for three and a very clear speaker. He said, 'She fell in the water and a man had to pull her out.'

Mother went mad and said, 'That's the last time you take your brother swimming. You can't even be trusted to do that properly.'

For once, George had done me a favour. I hated the swimming pool, with or without him.

Funny thing about George: no matter how I tried to avoid him he was always there in front of me or else trailing after me wanting us to play hide and seek or other stupid games. If I read a book or one of my Mother's magazines, he wanted to know what it was about. To get rid of him I'd put on a Hallowe'en gorilla false face that frightened the life out of him, but my Mother caught me in the act, burned the mask and slapped me as hard as you could.

'Do you want that child to die or something?' she demanded. I felt like saying, 'Yes, and you too.'

'She's only a child,' said Dad. 'She didn't mean anything.'

I knew he didn't care that I was only a child. All he wanted was peace at any price. I tried to keep out of everybody's road but it was difficult in a two-bedroomed flat. It was even harder when we were on holiday, lumped together on a beach with George throwing sand in my eyes as though it was a great joke, then following me around and shouting on me to wait for him while I ran away, pretending not to hear.

One sunny afternoon my mother asked me to watch George while they went for a game in the bowling green reserved for visitors. I said, 'But it's my holiday too. I want to play on the swings.'

'So do I!' said George, suddenly, at my side.

'You can play on the swings any time,' said my mother, so we were forced not to. I wondered why grown-ups bothered going on holidays when they only wanted to play bowls, but half an hour later I dragged George past the swings feeling quite happy. I had a ten-shilling note stolen from my mother's handbag and thought she'd never miss it as she seemed to have plenty left. In a shop I bought the dearest sweets I could see. They were called Chocolate Liqueurs and shaped like little bottles. We guzzled them down as fast as we could, then George was violently sick.

'I want to go home,' he said, as white as a sheet. We returned to the digs and sat on a couch waiting for our parents. I warned George to say nothing about the sweets but he immediately told her he was sick of eating chocolate liqueurs. She cried, 'Chocolate Liqueurs? They must have cost a bomb.'

She went to my jacket and took from the pockets loose change and two Chocolate Liqueurs stuck together, then told my Dad, 'To think I might have blamed the landlady for stealing and all the time it was her! We're going home.'

After that, George avoided me as if I had something infectious. It may have at last occurred to him that I was always up to no good, though the Chocolate Liqueur incident was forgotten, and I was left alone in the house while he went out and played with kids of his own age. I didn't hate him any more but didn't like him either. He was still my parents' favourite, while I was always doing bad things, and at twelve had begun smoking. When eighteen I married a handsome young man of nineteen in a Registry Office. My parents never came. They were right, I suppose. We were far too young and he was a heavy drinker. So I left him and took a job in a bar. It suited me fine. I liked the convivial company and had a few relationships, but had no intention of marrying again. I had no desire to be under somebody's thumb, and once bitten twice shy. With all that happening I lost contact with my parents and George too, who by now must be at least forty. I always meant to phone them but never did. I'd put my family to the back of my mind.

One morning I received a letter from George. He was in Australia – had been living there for years. It was a short letter, asking about my health and so on. *He* had not been well but was on the mend now, and though he loved most things about this big country he had bouts of homesickness. He missed his parents and me. He'd love to see us all, but couldn't afford the fare home. So would I please write to him; even a postcard would be appreciated. I read the letter more than once, letting it sink in. Then suddenly thought I'd fly to Australia and give him a pleasant surprise. It was the least I could do, so I did it.

The small town where he lived was not easily reached but at last a bus brought me there across a dried-up yellow plain that stretched as far as the eye could see. After some enquiries I was directed to a burial ground where George's coffin was lowered into a deep hole in the earth. At first I could scarcely speak to the minister in charge of everything, but finally managed to whisper that I was George's sister. He put his arm round my shoulder and I began to cry. I thought fate was very cruel to let me come all this way and find George dead. It was too much to bear.

'I never knew him really,' I told the minister, who now had his arm round someone else's shoulder. 'He was a young boy when I last saw him and now I'll never know what he looked like as an adult.'

By now the minister was shaking hands with the other mourners, who were mostly black people. I felt like an interloper who had no reason for being there. Then a woman wearing a man's jacket pushed her way through the crowd. Her face was kind and middle-aged and I was grateful when she asked if I was George's sister. She said she could see the resemblance. I asked, 'Did you know him well?'

'Oh, yes. He worked on our farm. He was one of our sheep shearers.'

That surprised me. It must have showed on my face for she said, 'And a very good one, too. He was a hard worker.'

After a pause she added, 'I'll give you a lift back if you want. My truck's over there.'

I said that would be fine.

As we got into the truck I thanked her, though I didn't want to go back. She said, 'You don't have to.'

'How do you mean?'

'Stay on the farm as long as you like. Get to know the place.' She laughed. 'Try a bit of sheep shearing yourself.'

I didn't say anything. I was too busy thinking. I finally asked where the sheep were because I couldn't see any. She laughed again and said, 'Don't worry, they wander off for miles at times but nobody touches them. There's no Ned Kellys in these parts.'

We passed the town and reached what seemed a stately but

run-down villa where she stopped the truck and got out, saying she was bursting for the toilet but would be out again in a minute. When she returned I told her that I'd stay for a short time, but pay for my keep.

'You'll do no such thing,' she said. 'You'll work for your keep. I need someone to clean. The last woman left. She was black and they don't stick long anywhere if they can help it.'

Suddenly I felt happy for no apparent reason. I had the strangest feeling that I would get to know all about my brother through this kindly woman and the vast country he'd obviously loved.

'I think I'll be sticking here,' I said. 'And do you know something? I've always wanted to be a sheep shearer.'

'You must be joking,' she said, and we both laughed.

Dilys Rose

In a TV programme attempting to define *What Makes us Human*, viewers were shown a painting by a chimpanzee which could have been – and was – mistaken for a Jackson Pollock. The marks on the page might have revealed something about the chimp's state of mind the day it took up the brush. Artists sometimes want to express/ explore/ exploit their feelings, but they do so within a cultural context, a particular palette.

A personal example. Some Brazilian students were given my story *Magnolia,* to help improve their English. Set in Edinburgh, the action revolves around a dilemma: a couple are moving house, want to take their cherished tree with them; will it survive being uprooted?

The students had to research any unfamiliar aspects of the story. Gardening was particularly weird for them, and we Brits even had TV programmes about it! In Brazil things grow, everywhere, all the time: avocados the size of grapefruit, grapefruit the size of melons, melons the size of footballs. The weather was also an unknown: cold dark winters, affecting plant growth and spirits? And what were tenements?

If anyone resident in Scotland read this story, they would get most of the cultural context. They'd know what a tenement was, that people get fussed about their gardens, are affected by bad weather. There are also references to the American Deep South, and a song called *Strange Fruit*, in which the scent of magnolia is overlaid with the smell of burning flesh from a racist killing. When I began writing the story I was thinking, very literally, about a tree which had been killed by builders doing renovation work. But these associations from elsewhere are also, essentially, part of my palette. Whoever you are, your palette extends beyond the borders of the familiar, whether we're talking nation or gender.

Dilys Rose's most recent book is *Bodywork (Luath Press, 2007).*

Dilys Rose

The Island Folk/Das Inselvolk

There is an island nation, itself a nation of islands, of fretted coastlines and perilous sea crossings, of shifting borders and debatable lands which was, from before the time of the Romans, invaded by many peoples and, in turn, did its own share of invading. It is a little island, with the silhouette of a hag, a carline, a crone or spaewife. It is cold and damp, with a number of even littler, even colder islands scattered around it, like handfuls of crumbs thrown from its shores.

This little island has always had ideas bigger than its station and, as the island folk say, eyes bigger than its belly. Its seafarers looked out from its ports at the grey waters around it and saw a great golden oyster of opportunity quivering on the horizon. In its heyday – and it was quite a heyday – the island folk, without a second thought, set out to sea – which was, then, the only option for islanders. Bearing firearms and trinkets and God on their side. If they found something useful to them – trading routes, political power, hot beverages, dangerous drugs, diamonds, oil, waiters, shopkeepers, doctors, sports people, etcetera – they hammered in their flag and took possession.

At the peak of its glory, the *pinnacle (*French from Low or Late Latin) or *zenith* (Old French from Arabic), people were fond of saying that the sun never set on the little island's empire. Imagine that! The globe bedecked with garlands of one's own fairy lights. A dominion of perpetual daylight – and heat – if one kept on the move. How reassuring for a little nation of notoriously bad weather to know that if one were to travel east, west or south from its native mud, one would eventually arrive at a place where the sun was baking its own diplomats, bureaucrats, managers and soldiers. A place in the sun. Another. How gratifying. What an enduring source of pride.

On a dark, dreary day at home, an armchair traveller might huddle by a sputtering fire and picture a clipper in full sail speeding across the ocean, any ocean, dropping anchor on some far-flung, sun-kissed shore, where the sweet sound of the little nation's national anthem, parroted by smiling barefoot children, might be heard drifting across a warm, *azure* (old French from

Arabic from Persian) sea. Of course, the little nation was also keenly interested in temperate climes and even frozen wastes; in fact a number of its adventurers were fatally drawn to the blinding whiteness of sun on ice.

The island folk were not the only ones who harboured dreams of expansion. Others, many from northern regions, were also driven to venture past the edges of the known world and stake their claim on *terra incognita* (too easy). Battles were fought between indigenous peoples and adventurers, between adventurers and adventurers. Deals were done. Dirty deeds were done. Continents were cut up and shared out, like pieces of pie. *(Can I have some more? Just a small piece for the moment, thanks.)* The interests of those who already lived there were rarely considered. Psychology was an issue. The minds of indigenous peoples didn't work the same way as the minds of the empire builders. For example, many of them didn't even consider land as something one could own! Or take away. Or have taken away. Until the fences went up and pffff! All gone. Ah well, the hardest lessons to learn are the most effective. Religion – oh yes, that was an issue too. And another hard lesson to be learned.

Time passed. Nations were renamed, reshaped. The little island maintained a sturdy imperial boot-hold throughout the sunlit world but after a while, the natives became restless. The jungle drums, the desert drums, the mountain drums and the plains drums all began to beat. The nights were full of rustles, whispers, the fear of *ambush* (Old French from mediaeval Latin). The natives were no longer content to clean out *latrines* (from Latin), wash the underwear of the plantation manager's gin-soaked wife, to don white gloves before serving up food at the master's table, to endure brutal punishment for stealing a banana to feed a hungry child. The natives had changed. They had become ungrateful, untrustworthy, devious, greedy – they wanted the tea and coffee, the diamonds and opium, the salt and oil for themselves! They refused to eat. They bit the hand that fed them. They talked about rights!

At first the island folk fought staunchly to defend their not always hard-won places in the sun, but the natives fought back and after a while, the island folk grew weary of insurrections flaring up all over the place. Distant territories were simply becoming too much trouble for the island folk, who were becoming tired of the big wide world. They preferred their own company, a quiet life, a chance to put their feet up, were ready to wash their hands of all imperial holdings and get back to what really mattered: watching the cricket, the rugby, the football, talking about the weather and filling their bellies with bland food. They were ready to become, once again, *insular* (Latin again).

But what's done can't so easily be undone. Their culture, religion, bureaucracy and, most importantly, their *language* (French from Latin) had travelled far and wide. Their language – what language? In the early days, the island was not *monoglot* – (from Greek) – though now the island folk are considered to be linguistically challenged. The island wasn't even a single nation for very long at all but many, then several, then two or four – depending on who you are – held in uneasy proximity by Royal Decree and the steely swell of a cold sea.

Even on home ground, those in control of the island folk liked things simple, straightforward and there was nothing straightforward about a populace speaking in different *tongues* (from Old Norse, Old German, Latin): it caused confusion, division and heavens, there was enough of *that* to deal with. The solution? One language for all. And those who wouldn't, or couldn't avail themselves of the official tongue had better get out of sight, and earshot, take themselves off to some windswept tail of the island. Better still, to one of the littler islands. Even better, pack themselves onto coffin ships bound for the edges of empire.

One might think that the adoption of a single language might suggest some deep and ancient affinity of tongue with soil but no, this language was an *import* (from Latin), *a hotchpotch* (from French or Dutch), a *mongrel* (Old English!), bred from the tongues of several invading continental tribes. Did this matter? No. The fact that other, older languages had dwelled there longer and in a purer state was not much of a consideration. Nor was the fact that the designated language was, frequently, not spoken by the little island's kings and queens. *Monarchs* (from Greek), like other commodities, were often imported, and could not or would not speak the language of the island folk.

But the language, a hardy plant, put down roots and flourished. The island folk found it to their liking – well, enough did and those who didn't ... that's another story. Once they had fully adopted the language and, in the manner of adopters, named themselves as its parents, they sent it back out into the world. What a lucky language it was. Why, without the island folk and their clipper ships, it might have dwindled and withered into some quaint antique dialect spoken by one or two tiny regions on the nearest continent. But no, it arrived, it thrived, it adapted. New varieties sprung up everywhere: in the *desert* (from French), the *jungle* (from Hindi) on the *prairies* (from French), the *tundra* (from Russian). It was a greedy language, soaking up new words through its roots, snatching them from the air, growing like a beanstalk, bigger and bigger.

There's an old story about a beanstalk. A boy, Jack, is sent to market to sell his poor mother's milk cow so they can eat. Instead, a stranger on the road persuades him to trade the cow for a handful of magic beans. His mother, in rage and despair, throws the beans out of the window and sends her silly son to bed without any supper. In the morning, Jack looks outside and sees a huge beanstalk. Being a curious boy, as well as a silly one, he climbs the beanstalk and at the top, finds himself in another world. First he meets an ogre's wife whom he persuades to feed him. Then he hears the ogre approach, his big voice booming out ahead of him:

> *Fi fie fo fum, I smell the blood of an Englishman*
> *be he alive or be he dead, I'll have his bones to grind my bread.*

Jack escapes being eaten by the ogre once, twice, three times, outsmarts him, makes off with his treasure, chops down the beanstalk, slays the ogre and lives happily ever after with his mother. The end. But what about the beanstalk? It was a magic beanstalk, after all, and magic plants tend to be hardy. What if, even though it had been cut to the quick, it sent out tubers in every direction? Soon there would be many beanstalks and at the top of each, another world, with its own hungry ogre.

Sheila Templeton

I live right by the sea, on the Ayrshire coast. I came here seven years ago. It's the only time I've moved house just because I longed to live in a particular place. Now, there are no job needs, no family needs ... though I love the fact that my son and his partner live in Glasgow and I see a lot of them.

This freedom to live wherever I choose probably sums me up. I feel free, now into my seventh decade, to be myself. Or as much of myself as I've yet discovered! And that frees me up to write.

I do find now a sort of linking-up going on in my process, a re-discovering of who I was as a child, in all that sharpness and colour. It's the TS Eliot 'coming back to where we started'. It's wonderful.

I don't know if it's the landscape, the changing light, magical Arran floating around the bay, or it being Burns' country ... but my writing has just taken off here, like the seagulls outside the window. My work is being published more extensively. I've discovered that I actually love reading my poems aloud. And this year I won two big prizes, the Robert McLellan and the James McCash Scots Language poetry awards.

Who I am today has been shaped by where I began. I had a nomadic and, in some ways, strangely fractured childhood, but the constant factor was always my grandmother in Aberdeenshire. Even now, I find myself pulled up North to that big sky, to surround myself with Buchan 'spik', to feel myself a child again. I always come back bursting with things to say, new poems. It's where I was born.

Last Train To Ayr, Saturday 24th March 2007

(Today's Football Result: Scotland 2, Georgia 1)

Nae space. The ticket attendant oot o his train, rinnin
up and doon Platform 13 pushin in ivery big belly
he can reach, so the doors'll close. Inside, ivery atom,
ivery molecule o oxygen needed for the singin.
The roar fae deep down in the belly.
Prood Edward's army sent hamewards that often
they must be birlin, thir heids spinnin.
Nae sooner are they hame than they've tae dae it a ower again.

This train is shakin apart wi the stompin.
Kilts shimmer and sway, nae room tae strut.
Windaes draped in gowden glory o Lion Rampant.
Some guerrillas sport cocky stetsons, Saltire-blazoned.
Sound gaithers like a rollin wave deep in the gut,
then crashes oan oor heids. The noise is burstin ma eardrums.

Wimmen keep their eyes doon, fearfu.
Best tae sit sma, catch naebody's glance.

A wee wifie bound for Prestwick International Airport
gets pulled in through the door at Paisley Gilmore Street
and pops out the ither end, through the tunnel
o legs an airms, her suitcase rolling ahint her like a pony.

We dinna look at her either. Eyes still lookin at the flair
for fear o the things that happen when men and drink
get thegither. But then, a maist mysterious thing happens.
Wimmen start tae peek oot fae unnerneath hair fringes,
coat collars. Sideways glances, jist tae mak sure.
Then gradually shooders cam doon. Chins come up.
Sisters, we're in nae danger here. We could bare breists,
shimmy bare nakit oan the tables. They dinna ken we exist!

And we catch each others' glance and smile and smile mair,
then laugh oot lood. Because it wis a stoater o a result.

Sheila Templeton

Tasting Stars

Stars are sharp salt tonight, the sky dark
with dreams. We dance in a bowl of light
from a street lamp, the pavement sparkling
under jiving feet. Music makes eyes at me,
breath smokes and crackles into a bouquet
of snow flowers. And a new wondering,
a salty question, a longing in the blood
to understand the wolf whistles, the words
curving and sliding out of dark corners, where
boys now whisper my name. I hurry past,
fearful. Yet knowing, in this frosty air,
something is coming. Dancing on the rim,
waiting. Fingers snap like frosty twigs,
blood pumps every wondering pulse.
Cold stars burn my throat.

Anne Macleod

We are living through an age of rapid and increasing change. Our cities expand in multi-cultural diversity. The way we live, the way we work, is daily more complex, more dependent on technology, on distant communication. Not that any of this is entirely new. History offers evidence of tide after tide of change beating on the shores of Scottish nationhood with the certainty and inevitability of time.

I too am an incomer: second generation. Born and bred in Scotland, yes, but of Irish and English parents swept here in the 1940s.

My mother had to leave school when her father died. Her Northern Irish family could not afford to let her complete her education. She came to Inverness at fourteen and worked on the buses till she was old enough to join the WAF. That's where she met my father, an electrical artificer. Newly demobbed from the Navy, he whistled at a tiny WAF scurrying from the shower block wearing only her greatcoat. Such moments change lives. They married and came back to the Highlands where my father found work on the Hydro schemes. There is scarcely a part of the west or north where he did not work, either on the dams, or later wiring houses, or setting up TV aerials.

Technology changes lives. As do people. My parents raised a family of five: a family that has gone on to work in medicine, in education, to be successful in business. Some of us left Scotland, are living in exile. Our work, our families, are more diverse than our parents could ever have imagined on that day in 1947, before they met, before they knew they were a couple, a family.

I find it difficult to imagine the shape of my children's lives even twenty years from now. I choose to live and work in the northern landscapes I find so beautiful and necessary. Will they? Will they stay in Scotland? In Europe? Will we be dependent on the increasing sophistication of technology for communication? Will they find satisfying work? Will the pension funds hold out? Will they ever be able to retire? They will, I hope, continue to write and paint and play with passion and dedication, as they do now. I wish them peace and flexibility. Stamina. And love. What changes?

Anne Macleod

Walking the Parapets

If you do only one thing in Helsinki, take the trip across the harbour to Suomenlinna.

Siri is told this by such different people – from the greying businessman beside her on the plane (lost in spreadsheets and figures, only looking up as they swoop across the coast towards Vantaa airport) – to the pony-tailed waiter in Aulanko who shows her where to sit to be shielded from the draught yet still retain the best view of the lake. The food is fish, healthily starred with bright redcurrants. The hotel reminds her of a student hall. This surprises her before she stumbles on the photographic collage of its Bauhaus past. Simplicity and function. Each room with its neat bed, tiny balcony and views across the forest. The glassed-in corridors would, in the past, have been opened to the elements, circulating air. Till Siri discovers the building's origins she is unable to appreciate its crafted minimalism.

The Spa is something other. She escapes to it each morning from the spartan luxury of her single room, treading the silent maze towards the horizon pool, finding it empty, its spreading waters warm as most jacuzzis but not, somehow, equivalent to swimming in a bath. Even the outside pool is comfortably warm. Floating on her back, eyes drawn by the mist rising from the lake, by the encircling birch flickering minute by minute, gold and deeper gold, Siri wonders at such unlikely reality.

Seven a.m. here in Aulanko. Five a.m. at home. At home she would still have been asleep. At home she would not waken till the alarm at seven-forty, raking her from sleep, pulled her – all unwilling – into the morning battle of family and work. At home she would have longed for even an extra ten minutes in bed. Here, she is awake. Too awake. Minutes drag to hours she cannot fill. Her papers for the meeting are in order. Her clothes, perfectly ironed, languish in her room. Without interruption, without the press of childish voices, make-up and hair take no time at all. Not even an extended session on the Auklanko's free internet will breach the yawning gap. She can't phone home. Too early. And breakfast itself is a lonely affair even with the solace of a book. There's no one to be coaxed into the day, shoe-horned into uniform, swept to school. No tantrums. No tears. No lunch boxes to fill with last minute treats. No forgotten homework. No school-run hitches.

How will Nathan manage?

She shakes her head. Nathan will have no trouble at all. Kathy will do everything for him.

'Are you certain,' her mother asks every week, 'that girl is all she seems?'

'What do you mean?'

'It's not natural,' her mother never stops at the question, 'to leave a man alone with children. Stands to reason.'

'He's not alone. Kathy will stay over.'

'That's what I said.'

Pregnant silence.

'She's their nanny. It's her job.'

'You're the mother. You're the wife.'

'Nathan's their father. And Kathy is the best help we've had in years.'

Her mother says nothing, raises an eyebrow.

'If I wasn't working, Mum, you'd be quick to criticise.'

'I'm saying nothing.'

She says nothing every week. Little by little, Siri's confidence erodes. When she phones she half-imagines Nathan sounding guilty, embarrassed, and even Rose and Sam defensive. At five and seven! She shakes her head, sending water rippling across the surface, steam rising to the autumn birch. She ought to leave the pool. The mist is rising, the Spa beginning to fill up. Even the outdoor pool is about to be invaded. Siri slips across the narrow space, ducks under the clear plastic curtains into the glassed-in heat. Tomorrow she'll be on the move, not home but to Helsinki. Nathan had agreed when she booked the trip that it would be sensible to take the extra day.

'Why fly all that way and not see the place? When will you get the chance again? I'll be fine. So will the kids. Kathy will cope.'

Kathy would, Siri knew. Her mother raised an eyebrow, saying nothing.

The book fair finishes today. Siri has the afternoon to see more of Aulanko. Tomorrow she'll explore Helsinki.

What was it they said – if you do only one thing, take the ferry to Suomenlinna? Perhaps she should do that. Showering, drying herself, padding the corridors in thin towelling slippers, she considers the trip.

'Gives you a perspective,' the man said on the plane. 'Best way to see Helsinki.' Odd that the best way to see somewhere in perspective should so often be to leave it.

Later, after lunch, waving her colleagues away, Siri feels drawn to the antique shop next to the hotel, the remnants of the former Aulanko mansion, now filled with generations of furniture and ornaments. Was this the original entrance to the building? It looks as if it might have been. Unable to read Finnish, Siri cannot tell. She admires the white board of the walls, woven in complex diamonds and capped by ceilings of inevitable intricacy: the long central hall roofed in ruby and yellow glass, chambers on either side unconventional in wood and plaster. The corner of each room hugs a large white stove cylindrical from floor to ceiling. Aulanko, the mansion, caught fire, burned to a cinder. Wood and stoves, it's clear, are not always a happy mix.

'En puhu Suomea, anteeksi. Englantia?'

Siri trots out the apologetic phrase. The boys in the antique shop respond in unembarrassed English, suggesting she spend her afternoon exploring the national park, walking the lake. A visit to the tower, perhaps? And for Helsinki tomorrow – 'Suomenlinna,' they chorus. 'Helsinki's pearl.'

There's nothing in the shop that catches Siri's eye, nothing to amuse Nathan, Rose or Sam, nothing that might travel in her suitcase, though the prices seem reasonable enough. She excuses herself, wandering out of the shop, down towards the shore. She has already climbed the tower, toiling the hundred steps through Rapunzel-like rooms to the rooftop beyond which the spreading forests of south Finland fledge a far horizon. She has seen nothing of the lake beyond the glistening water flashing light into the lakeside conference rooms. All week the changing birches have flared around it.

The skies are blue, untroubled. Siri strolls along the shore, past the Spa, past the old bathhouse beyond the hotel. Visitors to the park are playing golf, picking berries in the scrubby undergrowth between the golf course and the trees. Canoes dart through unruffled water. A concern of horses, led by young girls smart in riding jackets and jodhpurs, circles two fields where a pony event is in full swing. Allergic to horsehair, struggling not to breathe, face tingling, Siri ploughs on.

The lake is beautiful, perfectly still. Every corner she turns brings more houses, each one newer and more intricate than its neighbour. Every corner offers more expanse of lake. The boys had intimated she might walk around it: that clearly will not be possible. But she cannot believe how well grown the trees are in Aulanko, how fat the acorns spilling from the oaks, how cheerful the bark of the sturdy birches peppering the shore. She stuffs her pockets with handfuls of ample acorns. Perhaps she'll plant them, grow a Finnish oak at home. She pulls her collar up, feeling a little too solitary, feeling the air brisk and cold despite the cloudless sky. Her cheeks are freezing.

Home.

Deep in her jacket pocket, a hollow buzzing deepens to vibration. Her house number flashes on the screen.

'Hi? What is it, Kathy?'

'It's not Kathy. It's me.' Her mother, sounding tearful.

'What are you doing there? Where's Kathy?'

'I don't know. I came round like I always do on Thursday, to see Rose and Sam. Well, they're not here. There's no sign of them. No sign of that girl. No note. And nothing but abuse when I phoned Nathan.'

'You phoned Nathan in clinic?'

'What else should I do? I thought if they're not here there must be something wrong. It's Thursday. They're always here on Thursday. Expecting to see me. Waiting for their chocolate.'

'Leave it for them, Mum.'

'And miss seeing their faces?'

Siri sighs. 'What did Nathan say?'

'Nothing I could repeat.'

'Don't exaggerate. He doesn't swear. Wouldn't swear in clinic. Not with patients there.'

'I know what I heard. When next I see that young man he'll have a piece of my mind – and as for that so-called nanny – '

'She'll have taken them out shopping. Visiting a friend. Or – '

'But I always come on Thursdays.'

'How is Kathy to know? Thursday's her half-day! You never see her. She never sees you.'

'A better mother – a better *daughter* – would have warned her to expect me!' The phone slams down.

Siri shakes her head, tucks her mobile in her pocket. The sky is still as blue. Why is she suddenly so cold?

A few hundred metres ahead, a narrow trail snakes to the left, away from the lake. It might be quicker to go back that way, but it looks isolated, less open than the path that brought her here. She shivers, opts for speed. She is deep in the forest, making good time when her phone buzzes, raking the silence once again.

'Mum! What now?'

'Siri, it's me.'

Nathan does not sound like himself. Just three words, distorted by eight hundred miles of mobile. But there's something up. It's as if he's on the phone to patients. Or their relatives. She keeps walking, phone pressed to her ear.

'What is it?'

'I don't want to worry you,' his voice is thin. 'But there's been an accident. As far as I know, Sam and Rose are fine –'

'An accident?'

'The school bus turned over on the Glen road. There are injuries. At least a dozen kids brought into A& E.'

Siri echoes, 'An accident? The *school* bus?'

'The injured are already here.'

'And Sam and Rose?'

'No sign of them. We think we've all the casualties –'

'You *think*.' Siri has a sense of looking down on herself. Pale and small. Insignificant.

'You know how these things are. There may be others.'

She swallows, her throat a scree of broken glass. 'Where's Kathy? Kathy must have picked them up.'

'I can't get hold of her. She's not answering her mobile.'

'I'll raise her, Nathan.' Siri is amazed how calm her voice still sounds. It continues, soothing, 'They'll be fine. Of course they will.'

Silence stutters between them, stings like hail, like blizzard swirled to whiteout.

'Nathan,' she shivers, 'I'll phone you when I've reached her. Ring if there's any news. Now, back to work. Go on. Love you.' She snaps her phone shut. Stares blindly about her.

Leaves, green and yellow, smother the fading sky. Trodden gravel scours her feet. Brambles snatch and lacerate. Birch stifle, sullen, threatening. Siri collapses at the foot of a heavy, lumbering oak and rocks there, frozen.

Sam and Rose.

Rose and Sam.

Kathy.

Kathy.

She must phone Kathy. Where *is* Kathy? Kathy must know by now about the accident. The bus is never this late. She must have phoned the school, or the bus company. Or one of the parents, surely –

And Nathan, poor Nathan has to pull himself together, treat the injured youngsters, some of whom he'll know – any one of whom might be Sam or Rose, altered beyond recognition. No, Siri shakes her head again. Not *Rose. Not* Sam.

Nathan will manage. Of course he will. He will do his work diagnosing, healing – his hands, like a magician's, consoling damaged limbs. While she – so far away, she can do nothing. Nothing.

No. She can phone Kathy.

She *must* reach Kathy.

Siri's hands shake as she fumbles with her mobile. Across the world, almost a continent away, a phone rings out.

No answer.

Siri tries again. Sits for ten minutes, fifteen, thirty, doggedly redialing till it strikes her she is blocking her own line. She checks the screen – no missed calls. She texts *Phone me, Kathy, URGENT* – sends it winging through the ether. Struggles to her feet. The hotel cannot be far away. Surely she should see its soaring central block? Perhaps she should ask another walker?

But no one has passed her on this path.

Sam. Rose.

She must get back.

Hours later – it seems like hours – Siri stumbles in sight of the golf course. Then she's running, heart thumping, racing past the paddock where the last two or three horses stand munching grass; past the berry pickers' glade; past the sagging bath house. The hotel shines whitely in the trees.

She stops running, bending over, wheezing. How long is it since she's run so far, so fast? How many years since she gave herself a stitch? She straightens up, holding her side, conscious of a new vibration, not in her bones or muscles, but in her pocket.

Her voice is sharp as ice. 'Yes?'

'What is it, Siri? What's up?'

'Kathy! Where have you been? Are Sam and Rose okay? Are they with you? Did they both get off the bus in one piece?'

Kathy sounds bewildered. 'They're fine. What's this about a bus? Sam isn't fond of water, as you know, but he really liked the pool this time –'

'You've been *swimming*?'

'Is that a problem? I picked them up before lunch. Lied a little – said they had the dentist. I'd booked the smaller pool and Siri, it was *great* – so quiet – you should have seen them –'

Siri drops her phone, retches till there's nothing in her body, till she feels as empty and lacking in substance as the gathering cirrus in the fading sky.

Next morning, the Helsinki sun dazzles the white city as Siri boards the ferry for Suomenlinna. She sits outside, on top, behind the bridge, in the first row of ranked benches. She can see well from here, yet be sheltered from the breeze. The sparkling harbour waters are insensibly clean. No oil slicks. No floating rubbish. How can that be? Even clean harbours in Britain would look heavier, duller. Here, cruise ships and ferries rise like skyscrapers from the crystal waves, towering above the green and fertile islands.

The terraced beauty of Helsinki unfolds before her, and will remain before her all the day, while she walks the faded buildings and strutting parapets of the islanded fortress that is Suomenlinna. More than once, she'll find herself withdrawing from an edge, an unexpected sheer drop marked DANGER in Finnish she cannot translate. But in the wooden café she'll find echoes of Aulanko – the complex rusticity of the shuttering wood, the kindness of the owner, the excellence of the fish, the unusual and oddly disembodied antique dolls. The echoes of children dashing round the green sward by the school will make her ache for Rose and Sam (back to school, annoyed they missed the drama. *But Mummy! I could have had a plaster on my leg! Like Tom! And weeks off school. It isn't fair –*)

A young couple drinking coffee on the cliff will hold their tiny child, planning aloud its naming party, the young father reminding her a little of Nathan at that age. (Rose and Sam never had a naming party. Should she have another baby, another child to name, another child to gather in the circle of her arms, like that proud, careful mother?)

Siri will be glad to have seen all this, to have seen the main museum and its film outlining the history of the place, its beginnings, erratic progress, the slow build up to seeming impregnability, inevitable downfall. And in the best of the galleries (for this Suomenlinna is a synergy of guns and roses, art and military) she will discover fragile snow-petalled flowers strung on thread – invisible plastic twine, strong as love, binding the stream of white ceramic blooms. She will buy metres of this star-like ribbon, have it packed carefully for travel. She will carry it home, a Finnish curtain, draping variable lengths of it over every window till Nathan objects.

'It's not Christmas, Siri –'

She will leave the flowers shining, separated, strung together, swinging between parapets.

Siri will do all these things. For now she settles into the boat, hears the engine putter, gulls wailing, traffic in the city fading as they swing out through the Sound past tiny, deep green islands, dotted with houses, ringed by boats. The wood and metal of the bench support her, sustain this outward journeying, the ache of salt and oil strong in her nose.

In winter, she thinks, the Sound must turn to ice, a meadow of white rigid flowers.

A family of landfalls. A sea of pearls, connected.

Suomenlinna.

Dorothy Baird

Born in Edinburgh, I left the city to go to university in England, where I quickly became aware of my Scottish-ness: the subtle language differences, for example, took me entirely by surprise; 'tea' wasn't the evening meal and no-one understood what 'to do the messages' meant. Let alone words like 'slitter', 'glaikit', 'fankle' and 'puggled' – words that, thanks to my Airdrie-born parents, I had grown up with. I returned to Scotland after almost ten years living and travelling elsewhere, returning because, as one of the poems describes, during an illness I realised that my whole body simply longed to be back home, close to the hills and sea and that uniquely Scottish spirit of place.

Now I have three children, and making time to write is hard because it involves putting writing first. This of course means putting myself first – not something that seems to come easily to a woman, even less so to one who is a mother. Nevertheless, I am grateful I am a woman: the very emotional demands that make life so exhausting also allow me occasionally to catch inspiring glimpses of the wonderful richness of life.

As well as working on my poetry, I teach creative writing to adults in the community and in mental health settings. I love this work as, in the pleasure it so obviously brings, I am reminded how the creative process re-connects us with our humanity. I also work as a Human Givens therapist, a therapy that, amongst its many tools, uses metaphors and stories to help achieve mental health. And somewhere in the midst of all of this, I try to find time to read, go to the theatre, walk in the hills, see friends and even sometimes simply to sit and watch the tadpoles wiggle in the pond.

Dorothy Baird

Home Truths

In the West Midlands my body
wouldn't move. My throat
hurt. *Glandular Fever* they
said, and my voice croaked
as it tried to speak a truth
it was only just learning; as
a longing I didn't know
had shaped my bones,
now ached so deep I knew it
as a pulse, like an ancient lineage
reeling me in.

It would not be ignored.

I brought my weak limbs North
to rest beside the hills, the sea,
the islands thrown like chuckie stones
off crinkled coasts. I watched
the tides turn, the nub of a seal bob
and dip in waves, pinks grow
among rocks, felt the land
settle like a clean sheet
around my limbs, breathed
salt like medicine
in the constant wind.

Motherland

How can I ever say what Scotland
means to me when it is so much
part of me, like a child whose world
is a reflection of themselves, whose
mother is their body still, for whom
the sword of separation, the knife
of loneliness, has not yet fallen?
Though I have separated, have travelled
the loneliness of other countries, the landscape
of my self – always I return, like the gannet
spears the miles to its own ledge, the osprey
reads the air to its nest, the salmon tastes
in flowing water the unique river of home.

Dorothy Baird

What Does it Mean to be a Woman Living in Scotland?

It's arguing with my children over bebo
anticipating cold, sleet, smir, and being
astonished sometimes by sun
allowing myself the sinfulness of pride

abseiling through an argument
answering the phone from Bombay
aiming to grow old with a chuckle
abrogating responsibility for haggis

agonising over other people's noisy headphones
abandoning courgettes to slugs
abiding with a bidie-in
awaiting my comeuppance

abolishing the sinfulness of pride
aborting attempts to cross the Kingston Bridge in rush hour
accumulating pennies no-one wants
acquiring a mobile phone and never remembering the
number

aching with the knowledge of death
acknowledging Scotland is my home even if it's full of deep
fried mars bars
acting as if it doesn't matter when it rains
adapting to new summers

adjusting to a music collection I can't hold in my hands
admitting I'm wrong – but not very often
advertising Scotland's a great country apart from the midges
affecting an outcome by being alive

affirming we're a wee country that thinks big
agreeing with anyone for the sake of it
airing old arguments for the sake of it
alarming anyone who doesn't know how it is

appreciating the wind on Rannoch Moor
approaching fifty
assuming nothing
asking for answers to questions like this...

Dorothy Baird

Smothering Words

I'm a woman. I have hips and breasts.
And three children. And I love words.
I want to fling them in the wind
like washing on the line. Toast them
in the sun. Juggle them
to make my children laugh.
Often I can't find them. (Words
that is, not my children.) Because hips
and breasts mean mostly these children
are mine. And words get muddled
when you never finish a
thought. Because a tractor's flushed
down the toilet, raisins stuffed
in the teapot spout, a concrete step
bangs a forehead (with the lump
and tears to show for it). And though my learning curve
is sheer as the Bass Rock and inside I am wide
as the Moray Firth with all that growth
it would be nice, sometimes, to slip away
for a day or two, roll silence
like a poke of soor plooms
round my gasping tongue, find words
for the prickle of missing their small faces.

Anne Morrison

I wrote my first short story in 2000, squeezing in the actual writing between my work as a copywriter and my responsibilities as a parent. I've more or less stuck with the short story form since then, finding it versatile and satisfying. For me, the process of writing involves an unpredictable mix of heightened recall with the need to tell a story or document an experience. The story writes and rewrites itself in my head long before it ever hits the page.

I was born in the Western Isles in 1969, and I've lived in the Highlands and Islands most of my life. I left school in 1987, spent a gap year in the Netherlands, then took a degree in Religious Studies at Edinburgh University. After graduating, I worked in local government before buying a VW camper with the intention of absconding to Spain. Detours abounded. The van consumed petrol at a most alarming and ecologically unfriendly rate, so I sold it and swapped the road for the sea, working on a charter boat sailing to St Kilda. When the sailing season was over, I moved to the Scoraig peninsula in Wester Ross and my first child was born a couple of years later. After my marriage ended, I left Scoraig and my second son was born in Easter Ross. I now live in Lairg, Sutherland, with my sons and my partner, Sam. Focusing my energies on one place is very important to me now. It's possible to learn a great deal, just by paying attention and staying put.

Anne Morrison

Breaking Stones

My husband is looking at the mountains again, which means only one thing. In a few days' time, a week at the most, he will tidy his desk, pack a small rucksack and leave. He will head for the difficult slopes, the high ridges, places where he walks and wanders but cannot live. In order to live, he has struck a compromise with himself and with me, a compromise that has worked itself out in the form of a small house in the winter shadow of the highest peak of a twenty-mile wedge of Scottish mountain. Shunted awkwardly into the blue by a sideways shove of seismic proportions, the peak casts its shadow over us from November through to February each year. Sometimes, when the clouds refuse to roll back or the approach to the slopes becomes impassable with flood water, my husband travels to mountain ranges in other countries and comes back invigorated, expanded. Often, he finds that on his return the world is too full to talk about and so he cloisters himself in his study where he thinks and writes before growing hungry for altitude and elements again.

We have a son, Ben, named for the mountain that fills our eastern skies. Ben has never made the ascent of the mountain he is named for, being too heavy for me to carry all the way up and too slow for his father to keep patience with him. So for now, Ben and I are confined to a five-acre sweep of land extending from the base of the mountain to where the green land ends abruptly in ragged cliffs above a stretch of pale grey sand. Our world at the foot of the mountain, our world at the mouth of the wave.

We break stones. We started this now-routine activity by simply moving stones, but as soon as we'd accidentally cracked the first one open, there was no going back. Now we're forced to come up with all kinds of schemes to justify such intense, destructive work. We will build paths. We will devise underground drainage systems. We will uncover the coy face of a stone feathered with delicate fossil negatives. We will mine red and yellow seams of flaky ore and watch rock, hard-hit, deposit glittering mica and lumps of moon-white quartzite amongst the dull shards at our feet. We will make our labours useful by collecting treasures and distributing them throughout the world in return for what we must compulsively break, in return for what we are compelled to shatter. Ben has a pair of safety goggles and a mason's hammer, good-sized, and he pounds away with glee. I start out with a pinch bar because my self-appointed job is to lever the stones out of the ground where they are interfering with the symmetrical planting of the orchard, but I quickly abandon the pinch bar and replace it with a sledge hammer, eyes narrowing as the chips fly. It feels good to be breaking stones on a damp, chilly morning in February as we slide out from beneath the mountain's long winter shadow. I hit it in just the right place – *glock!* – and a stone splits asymmetrically along an invisible fault line, releasing the quick dry puff, the hot musk, of opened stone. I inhale sulphur, scorched silica, a taste of iron or manganese; a scent of blood or the beginnings of blood on the air. Each day, my blows become more accurate and my knowledge of stone, of the texture and taste of it, deepens.

A friend, Julia, visits us on Saturday mornings with cakes and pastries.

'Where's John?'

I pour coffee into two small china cups.

'The Pyrenees,' I say.

Julia is wearing a silver and enamel pendant, one of her own designs. She fiddles with it while she talks to me.

'Doesn't it bother you, all this coming and going?'

I rake around in the teaspoon compartment of the cutlery drawer for my best spoons, the apostle spoons.

'No,' I say. 'No, it doesn't.'

John's absence hangs over us like a cloud.

'What's he doing this time?' Julia reaches for the cream, a lily-shaped purple cuff brushing the frosting on the pastries. 'Another fact-finding mission? Another book?'

'Something like that,' I say.

'Don't you want to get away? Go off by yourself for a while?'

'What for?' I examine the tiny features of an apostle, bearded and serious, on the tip of one of the spoons. His arms are folded protectively across his narrow chest in piety or self-defence.

'You could go walking. Go to the theatre. Sit in a café and read a book.'

'What for?' I say again. 'There's so much to do here.'

Julia sips her coffee carefully. I notice she's had her hair coloured a rich, deep auburn. It suits her.

'Don't you get bored?' she asks.

'Not bored. Never bored. Every day here is different.'

'I know that,' she says testily, straightening her pendant and turning her gaze on her hands. Julia has beautiful long fingers and carefully manicured nails, two rings, no, three.

'Every day everywhere is different, Anna. That's not the point.'

Julia is having an affair. She tells me that her husband knows and doesn't really mind, so long as she doesn't leave him. It isn't the first time Julia has had an affair.

'It makes me feel alive,' she tells me with a sigh. 'It makes me feel ... real.'

'Doesn't it distract you from everything else?' I ask.

'From what? Relationships are everything.' She licks her finger and dabs at the fallen traces of icing sugar on her plate. 'The rest is just a backdrop.'

The logistics of Julia's affair interest me.

'Where do you see him? Isn't it awkward, finding somewhere to go?'

Julia smiles. She likes to talk about her relationships.

'Mostly we don't go anywhere. We talk. He calls me on the mobile from work. We text. Sex doesn't happen that often. Hardly at all, in fact.'

'What do you talk about?'

'Oh, what he's doing at work, where he's going that day, when we might get a chance to see each other. I just like to know where he is, what he's doing. Then I can get on with other things. If I don't hear from him, it makes me anxious. But what about you and John?'

'What about me and John?'

'All that time apart. Don't you ever wonder?'

'It's never crossed my mind,' I say, and Julia laughs.

'Liar.'

We make paths. In the beginning, there was no path between the house and the hen shed. There were grasses, knee-high and heavy with dew on the sunniest of May mornings. There were tall pale cuckoo-flowers, lilac-white and lilac-blue, bearing balls of froth the size of Ben's pinkie nail. Living inside these tiny light-refracting bubble-homes we found neat insects, froghopper nymphs, with busy mouths. We tried to imagine what it might be like to be a froghopper inside a home with so many round wet windows.

'Trippy,' I said. 'Kaleidoscopic.'

'What does that mean?' said Ben. 'Do froghoppers have eyes? I think it would be like living in a cloud, only not so high up.'

We have worn a flattened grassy path but still we walk carefully, circling squat clumps of rush and skirting the inquisitive, long-necked iris. We tread gently around the iris, between the rushes. We move lightly through the cuckoo flowers, the sapling birches, the leafy alder. We wear a path with nothing but our feet and our daily habit of collecting eggs, a path narrow as a sheep track, idling, green.

That night, John phones me from a callbox.

'It's been a great trip,' he says. 'The landscape is amazing.'

'That's good,' I say, 'I'm glad.'

'I've got a load of new ideas, valuable stuff. How are things there?'

'Good. We went to the beach. Ben got toppled by a wave, came up gasping like a fish. I thought he was going to cry. But he laughed.'

'I miss you,' says John. 'I love you. The money's about to run out. See you tomorrow or the next day.'

And the line goes dead.

The following week, John comes back. It's late and I'm in bed but I'm still awake, reading. I hear the old van rumble up the track like a barrow of bricks before coming to an abrupt stop in the yard at the back of the house. There is a moment of silence and then the slide and slam of metal doors, John's footsteps on the gravel. Ben is asleep next to me, his forehead damp with the sweat of deep sleep. I hear John fill the kettle before going outside again and I know he will go and check the ponies, check the sheds, make sure the hens are shut in, confirm to himself that everything is as it should be before he returns to the house. He takes longer than usual and I conclude that he has started smoking again. I switch out the light. Later, I hear him enter the bedroom, undressing in the darkness.

'Are you awake?' he whispers.

'Hmmm. Yes … no … yes.'

'Is Ben in the bed?'

'Yes.'

'Shall I move him?'

I reach out for John and he holds me tightly. His hands are cold but his lips are warm and passionate. I breathe him in.

'He might wake up,' I whisper.

'Okay,' says John. 'I'll sleep downstairs.' He holds my head gently in his hands and kisses my cheeks, my forehead.

We examine rubbish on the shoreline. There are always spent gun cartridges in a range of colours but mostly faded red. If you didn't know what they were you might think they were the casings of discarded cigarette lighters. We study foreign writing, mysterious as runes, on detergent bottles that have lost all of their soft squeezable-ness. The scour of the sea has made them tough and brittle, thick-skinned, covered them with hacks. Ben drops pebbles into nests of rotting seaweed, raising clouds of small, slow-moving flies. We build sand forts with driftwood drawbridges surrounded by bonsai woods of heather-root trees, miniature copies of the ancient oak forests of the west coast, styled by south westerlies, pruned by salt. A single loud boom sounds above the continuous rumble of the surf and we press on, erecting stone circles out of elongated beach pebbles, building burial chambers to house the fragile skulls of seabirds or rabbits. We let the tide rush in and take the settlements. We don't mind. It happens over and over again, civilisations raised and razed. The sea's advance is always different, the disintegration of the fort unpredictable. The waves suck and draw on the sandy foundations of the standing pebbles until concave teardrop shapes appear around the base of each one, running into the receding waves as the pebbles list and slide.

Elizabeth Reeder

The reasons I arrived in Scotland are not the reasons I stayed and will not be the reasons I'll return. Perhaps I stayed because I missed my chance to leave, because this place took my heart before I even knew it was on offer. This no longer matters because I'm no longer of one country. In Chicago, Lake Michigan defines east and everything somehow moves in relation to it, clearly edged and limited. In Scotland, we're never more than an hour or so from the sea, urban coast or desolate wild unheld edges which provide an oceanic rocky sandy littoral space within which and beyond which my creativity freely moves.

Elizabeth Reeder

Passage Migrant

Writing Home, April 2006

I'm not sure how I feel about home any more. I'm not sure I'm needing a home at the moment. What I need is a stretch of coast and a flat bit of rocky grass. I need to be walking, wandering, rambling. The sea right there, light bouncing off the surf. Everything in that moment, the space between me and the sea. It's the up down, weaving in and out, cliff walking, dropping into bays, scrambling up rocks again. Where you don't know what you'll find. We're at Achmelvich where ten years ago we saw otters and a great northern diver on my birthday. This year it's mergansers and the first breeding pair of red-throated divers of the season. And it's windy in gusts again, unexpected calm and bracing wind. Walking with Amanda and Lesley and Della, our legs tired from walking up Conival in the snow, and I'm not particularly steady on my feet but I could walk for hours and hours but the others want pie and coffee and a nap so we turn around and head for Lochinver. And I'm desperate to be out, desperate to be blustered by the wind, to stand and see the sea, see everything.

This place feels like Oldshoremore did in November last year, when I was a mess and sat in the dunes unable to stop crying while everyone else played in the cold sand, wind-whipped. Or years and years ago, in a stormy February, Amanda and me walking the disused Cairngorm rails in a snowstorm when a peregrine shocked apart a winter protection of finches. These places take me to myself. I'm going to need this when we pack up and move. This feeling of standing at the edge of land, and it's a land that's rocky, unforgiving, graceful and generous. It's hard to be here. And the easiest thing in the world. I wonder if what I feel is only a small, small sense of what natives feel for this land. Does it drive others to tears? How embarrassing, how defining.

This is what I will take with me. What I will leave to come back to. This, this space of time, is not about things, not about a physical home, it's about this physical space of my body, who I take with me, who I move towards, it's the intricate twist of landscape and self and it's what will sustain me when I'm living on Fremont Street two blocks from Wrigley Field in Chicago, after I've moved back to the Midwest to fulfill some undefined urge to be close to my parents, to feel the emotional pull of these people, to be in the place I grew up, and there I will sit and I will write about home. For now I'm walking.

Running up to the Edge of a Cliff in Hurricane Winds, Storr Lighthouse, 27th of April 2006

Go Go Go Go Go. I'm breathing hard, my face pure red. My arms burning, pumping. My ears burn too, who's talking about me? It's the gulls, the gulls squawking: Look at that girl she's running, she's thinking she can fly, silly girl. And I don't care. Let them chatter. The gannets are kinder, brought into shore by the storm. They're diving, diving long bills, pale yellow heads, and the black tips of their wings, tucked in tight as they plunge through the air. I want to dive like that. From flight, in flight. I'm running so hard, go go go because the wind pushes up off the water, gale force, and it's not against me, it just is. The wind being wind. Birds, being birds. And I'm. Well, I run, run, run, my legs all there. It's a powerful stride and I'm out, out, out over the edge and the sea below is all foam and white and churning and I'm in the air, I'm in the air and I'm indefinable, I'm flying and I'm perfect and I stretch my fingers, tipped by light and shadow and there's a hint of pure sleek gannet black to them, and the wind is all powerful. And I'm out in the air, about to dive, and I'm flying, and it's impossibly blue, the wind slaps against my grin, grins with me and I'm me.

The Summer of 2006

We dismantle a home. We forget how to talk to each other. I spend four weeks out of seven travelling. We are fractured as we move together. We move from Glasgow to Chicago with four items of luggage, and 87 kg of boxes shipped.

As We Migrate

In Chicago, there's this bird lady and she saves birds, you know, that hit high buildings. The skycrapers turn off their lights for three weeks during the autumn migration and she collects flummoxed birds in the morning, the ones for whom lights-off was not enough, because there's still reflective glass, or glass that lets you aim towards hoped-for trees. With a butterfly net in hand, at dawn, she traps the birds she finds stunned at the base of the buildings and puts them into paper lunch bags. Distressed wild dry flutter rustle in bursts, like someone drowning coming up for air.

–

–

–

Two hours later, still that sound. See how ugly that tall sleek building is? See how it cuts a proud profile into the sky? See how if you didn't know the terrifying possibility of these buildings you'd be in awe as you flew past.

Driving Back to the Apartment, November 2006

The fact is that in the middle of an emergency the glimpses of beauty are almost accidental. Driving back to the apartment yesterday, after seeing my dad in intensive care, the lake churned up algae green and concrete grey, the waves coming in from the northeast and the wind explains why we were so cold last night. A winter lake, pre-freeze, all the boats in the harbours gone, small stubs of piers. And space. Winter gives vistas. Bare branches, spindly into the ice blue sky, and the sun so clearly defining what is there and what is absent.

The Healthy One (Novembers)

Dad is still slurring his words, so out of it that he doesn't take any of his meds on his first night home from the hospital, his skin hanging off him and yet, he's still puffy, his memory affected, his breath, halted, cut off. His short gait, uneven, and I can see the straight pain shoot through the roundness of his hip joints. His legs which he insists aren't retaining water, are, nonetheless, hardly bending at all on his way up the stairs. His left leg goes first. His right follows. Six half, halted breaths per step, not like he's been asked to do it – in through the nose out through pursed lips to give him more oxygen – and I'm worried about him by the third step. Worried because he's too heavy for me to stop if he staggers backwards, or if he stalls. Seven more stairs to go. And then five. And then a dozen flat shuffled steps to the folding chair unfolded in front of his bed. His stride is shorter than it used to be. In two months time, after my mom's had surgery, when she can't move her head on the bed, or when her hands shake so much she can't put on her glasses, or hold a glass of water steady enough to drink, he'll say he's the healthy one.

December 2006

Don't ask me about home. I've got too many, not a single one. I keep waking up while walking and living, like coming into consciousness, but just sharp into focus and keep saying, I'm in Chicago. I keep waking up from deeply restless sleep not knowing where I am.

Buildings Define the Space of the Street, January 2007

My dad nearly died when he was forty-nine: heart attack and triple bypass; blood clots in his legs. Another heart attack: Halloween; Christmas & New Year; Valentines Day. The bypass graft didn't stick and he was given no more than five years to live. That's the fact of it. I was fifteen and yet here he is twenty-one years later and there's nothing but joy in this fact. Except now my mom's health is faltering, my mom who has lived her life thinking that one day she'd be able to live her own life: free of kids and free of this man, a good man who takes up too much of the horizontal surfaces of her house with papers and magazines.

Yesterday a peregrine split a halo of pigeons wide open. Daring dives between the buildings of Ashland Avenue, the speckled lines of its tail clean, beautiful, honing in on the dirty grey spread of pigeons, the predator's eyes on a slow one, down, fast slice to the side, and up and out of sight. Those pigeons live on top of the car park, and I watched, they didn't settle for ages. They flew around and around looking more like starlings, the smaller dark mice with wings. On the wing. On the wing when their cluster was split wide open.

19th November 2007

Mom found Dad lying on his bedroom floor. 11:30 am and we have no idea how long he'd been lying there. He didn't respond when she shouted his name. To get into the room she had to force his leg to the side with the door. His c-pap machine blowing oxygen out of the mask into the air of the room. She'd already dialed 911 and Dad said, 'Karen, don't call 911.' She hung up. 911 phoned her back, 'Do you need help?' 'Yes, I think I do,' and the paramedics came. Forty-five minutes later, when I meet them in the ER, his eyes are thick with yellow mucus and he falls in and out of consciousness. Family is place. This is why we're here. I sit by his bed, hoping he'll recover, and in me I hold a country, a memory of Assynt which acts as a corset around my ribs as I try to catch a breath, any breath – the loch with a boat attached to a red buoy on its barely rippled surface, the heather brown hills beyond brought low by thick mist, leafless rowans clinging to the edge of the water. I've been know to cry out there, like I've been known to cry in the Rothko room at the Tate, or in the car with the music blasting as I drive once again to the hospital.

This Place I Come Back To

I'm naked, but for a pair of boots – fell runners, but higher – big, thick socks. Right. There. I'm standing back. Night will fall fast tonight, the pulses of three lighthouses breaking through the dark. Here it's still bright and I'm thin but not skinny, face red from the running I've already been doing. Red thighs too, from the wind, the slap of cold; you see me half-way there, briefly from the front, you see how my face is thin, tight-held like my mom's, how my hands are expressive and knuckly like my dad's, and then from behind, strong legs, you see the strength there, the dancer's posture, the hair that needs cut, it whips. I run run run. I get smaller. I look more clothed the further away I get. Part of me disappears into cloud, part is earth. I leap. For a second I am sky and then I'm gone.

Cynthia Rogerson

The miracle is that I write anything at all. I put off writing till I have done every single thing I can think to do, including lots of unpleasant things, like cleaning the bathroom and talking on the phone and watching very bad films.

Being a writer in Scotland is probably easier than in lots of other countries, because of the weird weather. To be driven indoors by darkness and freezing rain, and then yanked back outside by luminous light, rainbows and uncannily warm breezes – well, it's a moody place, isn't it? Moods are good for writing. And long dark winters are especially good.

Not sure that being a woman writer is different from being a man writer. When I'm in full throttle (after the cleaning and talking and watching of films, etc) I don't feel like either. Which brings me to a very good reason to write: I get a break from my self.

The Long Missing

She had just emerged from what felt like a very long sleep, but was in fact fifteen years of marriage. She noticed, in a detached way, that she was on holiday with her children. They were all in a caravan on a west coast beach, with the rain either hammering on the roof, or sailing by enclosed in tight dark grey clouds. In between, it was uncomfortably hot. The bay was shallow and the water heated quickly. Jelly fish in their hundreds were beached by the receding, deceiving sea. Whether it was raining or not, her children spent most of the days in the water, or on the beach, digging endless deep pits. They seemed tireless, and not at all concerned about the slippery jellyfish underfoot, or that their pits and dams had no purpose. The tides always undid their efforts, and they never cared.

It had not been a bad marriage, but deep down she had always felt they'd been frauds. From the outside, normal, but on the inside – quite often nothing, really. Not what she imagined should be there. Just two strangers rubbing along, pretending they weren't disappointed. Sometimes bickering, sometimes being grateful, but most often ... well, it was odd living with someone who would never really know her. She had always assumed something would happen to make it stop, and in the end something did. She'd felt almost numb with relief at first; then giddy as if she'd miraculously survived a horrendous car accident – one that had seemed inevitable. A drunk driver, black ice, a bad mood. She hadn't loved her husband after all, ever. Really, she hadn't.

Now she was here, uninjured, with the rain and the beach and her children, edging into a new way of being. She felt untethered, light, and continuously nervous. As if she was an actress who had not quite learned her lines.

He was with his sons, in the caravan next to theirs. A small man; dark and muscular and he moved like he loved movement. Like a dancer. Her children and his blended into one tribe, after five minutes of skirmishing around a campfire lit by some teenagers who ignored them. Everyone on the site was slightly shy around the teenagers. They were at once so beautiful, and so unbeautiful. Some were skinny with bad skin, and some were overweight and short. Even the prettier girls had glaring flaws, like thick glasses or fake tan lines, but no one could look at the teenagers very long without wishing they were fifteen again. Every night, they peeled off from their families, to drink gin and vodka and beer and smoke joints, by their fire on the beach.

She watched this fire, this mating beacon, from her caravan, and when her children were not back by bedtime, she wandered down to the beach to look for them. It was difficult walking in the damp sand in the dark, so she slipped her shoes off and squinted to distinguish her own brood from the other shadows of children. They all seemed to be racing towards each other, and screaming with terror. She listened carefully for crying and heard none.

Where are they? she asked him, this dark dancing stranger who lived in the caravan next to hers. Do you see my kids?

He had to lean in close to see her, and he said: There they are. Look! They're having fun. Let's leave them a while longer. They're playing British Bulldog, I think.

His voice in the dark sounded so intimate and pleased, as if he'd known her a million years and liked her inordinately. His teeth shone, and she could smell his skin. Warm and sweaty and something else. Well, he smelled of himself. A man she didn't know at all but liked. She let her eyes close momentarily. She told herself that intimacy had little to do with shared experience or memory. It was something much more visceral. If it was not easy, like this, then it was not right, and no amount of good intentions or indeed, children, would ever right it. Her marriage had been a fluke, a wrong turning; the kind of mistake that is easily made.

Much later, after all the children had been gathered like tired puppies and had their teeth-brushings witnessed, she drank beer with him by the fire. The teenagers had moved on to the privacy of dunes. The two of them leaned closer and closer, telling secrets, almost touching heads. Opening more beer, till she hardly felt herself. She watched his mouth as he talked. His lips, soft and thick. Her husband's lips had been thin.

The sea at ebb tide was black and still, and there was just a sliver of moon, but still their bodies shone pale as they slid into the water. How can the ingredients for happiness be so simple? Why was the sea not full of smiling, naked bodies? The shock of swimming in the freezing Atlantic felt like life was condensing around her. She gasped and sucked in her breath and didn't say anything to the man, too full of: Alive! Now! She suddenly saw all the days of her life as if they were boxes bobbing on the sea next to her. Some were open, and some were waiting to be opened, and they all had the same capacity – the same number of hours and minutes inside. But they were not the same, because today, this box, held an eternity. Not really, of course; that was the trick. Knowing that in a minute she would leave the sea, and this would be a memory too, made her heart and throat swell. I'm here, she whispered to no one. To everyone. To everyone who had ever lived, and who was homesick for life.

They stumbled out of the sea, and her skin was tingling but not cold, and she wrapped herself in his coat and kissed him, this dark stranger, as if it was her first kiss. She'd wanted to be in love for such a long time, she could not imagine getting tired of these salty kisses that tasted of midnight swims and beer. Later, his skin on hers felt smooth and cool, and she kept thinking how he was not her husband.

But she'd forgotten how love goes.

How first kisses are always last kisses. They have to be; when the sun comes up, they change into something more ordinary. And she began the long missing of her husband.

Janet Paisley

In 1950, a shy Scotswoman in London bought single railway tickets home for herself, husband and three daughters aged four, two, and baby – and for his girlfriend. She earned the fares cleaning other houses while pregnant. In Scotland, she lodged man and lover with her friend, said she was staying and he could please himself. A small inheritance meant she also bought two single fares back to London. That was my mother; me the two-year-old.

My family are Scots, mainly Highland, with one Norwegian grandmother. Dad's from Balloch, Mum from Avonbridge, where I grew up. We lived with her father and younger brother till he married, in a house full of books. Shooting, fishing and a vegetable garden fed us. Mum took in sewing to earn money. We spoke Scots, learned to forage, use guns, chop sticks, wire plugs, mend fuses, think for ourselves, depend on no-one – and to read. We read at mealtimes and in bed.

Mum was strict and deferred to no-one; nor was that expected. My grandfather was a paedophile, but feared her finding out. Raised to the refrain of universal equality – we're aw Jock Tamson's bairns – I didn't notice education taught no achievements by Scottish women: no books, art, science, history. The subliminal message was of a male world. Adult life saw that brutally enforced.

When I challenged male violation of women and children, the legal, medical, religious and political set-up supported it. My voice wasn't heard. Women didn't count. I opted out, raised my six sons alone, and wrote. I like men, but wouldn't marry one. I like women, but they tear each other down. I'm a writer, thrawn enough to write in every form, a product of this culture. Gender is still irrelevant unless I take a man to bed.

www.janetpaisley.com

Refuge

Refuge – the play is set in a living room, with phone, table, sofa, chairs, a large window on rear wall, exit to kitchen one side, exit to hall other side. In the hall, the main door is locked, chained, barred with bolts top and bottom – a veritable fortress.

Extract 1.

AGNES: (*sitting knitting*) You shouldnae wind Carolanne up like that.

SADIE: (*ironing*) She shouldnae crank up sae readily.

AGNES: (*stretches, rubs her ribs to ease pain*) Still an all. Same boat, ye ken.

SADIE: Different bloody river, but. (*banging with iron*) Aye, aye, I know. Still an all. (*pause*) You aw right?

AGNES: Just ma lumbago playin me up.

SADIE: Arthritis. Ye should say arthritis. Naebody says lumbago these days.

AGNES: Ah like lumbago. (*slowly*) Lumbago. Soonds better. Like dirty dancin.

SADIE: Lambada. (*dancing with sweatshirt she's ironing*) Dirty dancin. The Lambada. Oh, hey, I could get intae this. Give us a Smoochie wan, handsome. (*mock kissing*)

Carolanne enters with 3 mugs on a tray, stops, irritated by Sadie's nonsense.

CAROLANNE: Could you go suck your washing somewhere else?

SADIE: (*to sweatshirt*) Hey, pal, you got an ugly friend for ma ugly friend?

CAROLANNE: As long as he's not legless like yours. (*hands out tea mugs*)

SADIE: Legless? (*checks sweatshirt to see*) Ach well, so much fur the lambada.

AGNES: (*to Carolanne*) You wur quick.

CAROLANNE: The kettle never gets a chance to cool down.

SADIE: Didnae take time tae put a cloth oan that tray, but.

CAROLANNE: (*freezes, terrified*) Oh.

SADIE: Joke. Joke. Look, I was – okay, bad taste. But a tray, fur god's – fur three mugs? (*bangs the iron down*) Jees, I didnae mean it, right? Och, hell. (*lights a cigarette*)

(*Carolanne immediately empties the ashtray*)

SADIE: Wid you please no dae that? Everytime I light up.

CAROLANNE: You'll need an ashtray.

SADIE: I kin yaise a dirty ashtray. Whit's the difference. Ash, mair ash. It's aw fag ash. Let it alane till it's full, kin ye no?

CAROLANNE: (*puts ashtray beside Sadie*) It won't hurt you to use a clean ashtray.

SADIE: Naebody's coontin the fag ends.

CAROLANNE: It's just habit.

SADIE: My eye. Like yer supposed tae book?

AGNES: Hard tae gie up, habits.

(*Sadie tips ash from bin back into ashtray*)

SADIE: Trainin, that's aw it takes. Trainin an will power. Whit dae you think, Agnes? Am I no right?

AGNES: Weel, ah never kent dirt get annoyed, however much ye ignore it.

SADIE: (*to Carolanne*) See. One fag end already in ashtray. Noo watch this. (*with ceremony, taps ash into ashtray*) Nae lightnin. (*looks*) Nae Thunder. (*listens*) Noo I'll just ignore it and (*rests cigarette in ashtray*) get oan wi the ironin.

CAROLANNE: Why are you doing that?

SADIE: It gets the wrinkles oot the clothes.

(*Sadie bangs away. They are all uncomfortable, especially Carolanne*)

SADIE: Och, go oan. (*picks her cigarette up*)

(*Carolanne takes the ashtray, empties it, replaces it*)

SADIE: Feel better?

CAROLANNE: (*going back to her coffee*) Makes no difference to me.

AGNES: This is a nice cup ae tea, hen.

(*Carolanne is looking in her bag again*)

CAROLANNE: You're welcome.

AGNES: Husnae turned up yet?

CAROLANNE: No. I can't think.

AGNES: Maggie'll have put it awa, maist likely.

CAROLANNE: I expect so.

SADIE: Fur goodness sake. Gordon widnae touch your money.

CAROLANNE: I never said...

SADIE: (*cutting in*) He's no that kind.

CAROLANNE: I know. I just can't remember...

SADIE: A fiver. I mean, whit would he want wi a fiver? I'd know if he was spendin money he didnae huv.

AGNES: Naebody said...

SADIE: No, but you're baith thinkin loud enough.

AGNES: Least said.

CAROLANNE: Maggie probably picked it up before she left.

SADIE: An if she didnae?

AGNES: It'll aw come oot in the waash.

SADIE: No fae Gordon, it willnae. I'd stake ma life oan that laddie. Huv done. (*bangs iron down and goes to window*) Oh, see this place.

CAROLANNE: Mistakes happen.

SADIE: An that's aboot aw. Naebody visits. Naebody comes tae the door. There's a phone there an it never rings. Even the postman walks past. Whit aboot ma hoose?

CAROLANNE: Maggie will bring that. When it comes.

SADIE: It's like we're no here.

AGNES: But we're no here.

SADIE: Still, the postman could come, the phone could ring.

(*the phone rings. All three stare at it*)

AGNES: The phone's ringin.

CAROLANNE: (*to Sadie*) What did you do?

SADIE: Do? I didnae *do* anythin.

CAROLANNE: Answer it, then.

SADIE: Me?

AGNES: It wis your idea.

SADIE: I'm no touchin it.

CAROLANNE: You answer it, Agnes.

AGNES: Aw naw, it'll no be for me.

SADIE: It cannae be for ony of us.

CAROLANNE: Well, we can't just let it ring.

SADIE: (*to Agnes*) Whit ur we supposed tae dae?

AGNES: S'never done that afore.

CAROLANNE: Somebody should do something.

SADIE: You get it, then.

AGNES: Aye, go oan.

CAROLANNE: What if it's the school?

AGNES: (*to Sadie*) Mibbe Gordon's no weel.

SADIE: They'd ring the office.

AGNES: Weel, it's gein me the jitters.

CAROLANNE: Oh, I'll get it.

SADIE: No, wait. Maybe it'll stop.

(*phone stops ringing*)

AGNES: It's stoapt.

SADIE: See.

(*they resume their activities*)

AGNES: Wisnae fur us, then.

SADIE: Naebody knows we're here.

Extract 2

(*door knocker knocks*)

AGNES: Shoart walk. Mustae chainged hur mind. (*picks up her knitting*) Kin you get it, hen?

(*Beth exits. Agnes sits back, knitting. Gordon enters*)

AGNES: Aw, it's you, son.

GORDON: Eh, Agnes, Beth got the door.

AGNES: She'll dae aw right.

GORDON: Right.

(*Beth enters, skirting Gordon to go to the kitchen*)

GORDON: Right. Mum upstairs?

AGNES: Oot fur a walk. She'll no be long.

GORDON: Oh. Well, I'll get something ... (*turns for kitchen and stops, reluctant to go through because Beth is in there*)

AGNES: Ay hungry, eh?

GORDON: Aye. Yes. Is my mum alright?

AGNES: Sure, she's fine. (*pause*) Naw. That's no right. She wis a wee bit upset. Carolanne went hame.

GORDON: Because of me?

AGNES: You? Dear lord, awbody in this hoose is jist dyin tae take the blame. Furst yer mither, then Beth. Noo it's yersell. Whit herm did you dae Carolanne?

(*Gordon can't answer*)

AGNES: Come oan, spit it oot. Nuthin soarts fur bein kept in. Whit did you dae? (*gentle prompt*) Weel?

GORDON: Took her money.

AGNES: (*correcting him*) Stole her money.

(*Gordon becomes agitated, as if a dam burst*)

GORDON: I was going to pay it back. I didn't mean ... She didn't need to go home. I didn't think she'd miss it. Now she'll get ... that wasn't meant to happen. I would've paid it back, Agnes.

AGNES: Here, steady oan, son.

GORDON: I just didn't know what else to do.

AGNES: Noo look. Ye taen mine tae an I'm still here. Gied me ma pension short last week. Didn't ye?

GORDON: I'm sorry, Agnes. But you wouldn't leave. You never go outside. Does my mum know? Where is she?

AGNES: She's aw right. Calm doon noo. Yer mum kin look efter hersell.

GORDON: No, she can't. You don't know. The things my dad ...

AGNES: I know aboot yer faither.

GORDON: No, you don't. She never tells. Only bits. She doesn't want you to know how bad I am.

AGNES: It's no your shame, son.

GORDON: It is. She can't have a bath because of me. Only has a shower or washes at the sink. He held her under, one night. I tried to stop him. He was too big.

AGNES: You wur a wean.

GORDON: I was fourteen. When we left. The night before, he ... he went crazy. Tore her clothes off, in the living room. Said terrible things ... called her ... names. Said she was an ugly cow and ... and stuff. He made me sit ... on the sofa, stay ... and listen. He walked round and round and round, sneering. She tried to cover ... up. He ... slapped her, made her stand ... made me stay. Even when she needed ... the toilet. Wouldn't let her. It ran down... He wouldn't let me leave. My mum... I didn't know what to do. The way she looked at me. Her face all... I hate him. Wanted to ... make him stop ... wanted to smash his face in ... hurt him back and and ... I didn't ... move ... do anything. I was ... scared, Agnes. I was too scared.

(*Beth enters with baby's bottle and stops*)

AGNES: It was yer faither daen wrang, son. No you.

GORDON: I hate him. Soon as I'm old enough I'm going to get a gun and go find him. Then it'll be his turn. Then he can be the one who's scared.

(*front door knocker knocks*)

AGNES: That'll be yer mum. (*to Beth*) Wid you go, hen?

(*Beth sits bottle down and exits*)

AGNES: Listen, son. There's a road fur you tae go an hatin yer faither isnae it. Hate is haudin oan tae whit we're feart fae. Let it go. Let him go. Fund yer ain road.

GORDON: I will. When I shoot him. Once he's dead.

AGNES: He's deid awready, son. Think aboot it. Whit kinna life is he livin? Wid you want tae be inside his hert, inside his heid?

(*Beth comes back into the room carrying a bouquet of flowers. She is terrified*)

AGNES: Oh, hen.

BETH: Take them off me. Take them off me. Take them off me.

(*Gordon takes the flowers. Beth sinks to her knees but her arms stay out, as if still holding them*)

AGNES: Whaur did they come fae?

GORDON: (*to Agnes*) Her husband?

AGNES: (*getting up*) No at the door?

GORDON: No. It's shut. They must have been delivered.

AGNES: Ye shouldnae huv opened the door, lassie.

(*the door knocker again. It frightens them all*)

BETH: (*a whimper*) Oh please.

(*Gordon gives flowers to Agnes*)

GORDON: I'll go.

AGNES: Dinnae open it.

(*he exits. Agnes doesn't know what to do with the flowers*)

BETH: I didn't lock the door.

AGNES: Aw, jees. (*dumps flowers on her chair*)

BETH: I didn't lock the door.

(*Agnes rushes to shut living room door, pressing herself against it. Upstairs the baby starts to cry as Beth hides behind sofa, repeating that she didn't lock the door and Agnes, afraid, speaks over her.*)

AGNES: Aw, hey, Gordon'll no let him in. Nuthin'll happen. Nae danger. (*goes to stand in front of Beth, shielding her*) We'll be aw right. We'll be awright.

(*Sadie enters*)

SADIE: Whit the hell's aw the racket fur?

AGNES: Sadie!

(*in background, from hall, the sound of Gordon locking and bolting the door*)

SADIE: An the door no even locked. Whit's up wi hur? Somebody been waving their nick-nacks aboot again? I thought she'd huv shut up by noo. Cannae go oot fur five meenutes but…

(*her voice tails off as she sees the flowers*)

AGNES: (*to Beth*) It's Sadie, hen. It's only Sadie. Look, look.

(*Gordon enters*)

GORDON: Mum. It was the flowers. They're from…

SADIE: (*cutting in, in panic*) Who? Who ae they from? (*grabs flowers*) He cannae know we're here. In the name of god. (*finds label*) Who ur they fae? (*rips label off, reads. To Gordon, relieved*) Andrew. (*then, as comprehension dawns, looks over at Beth. Almost soundless*) Andr…

(*Beth is still whimpering, hanging onto Agnes*)

SADIE: Oh whit. (*hesitates then rips label into pieces, brightly*) Whit a relief.

AGNES: Relief?

SADIE: Aye. Fur a minute I thought they were fur wan ae us. The noise gaun oan. And here they're fur … fur … Carolanne! (*to Agnes*) Fur Carolanne.

(*Beth stops whimpering and looks up*)

AGNES: (*puzzled*) Carolanne?

GORDON: But she's gone home.

AGNES: (*trying to correct Sadie*) An hur man…

SADIE: (*cutting in*) Wid huv ordered them this morning. Before he phoned.

BETH: But the man … the man said…

SADIE: (*cutting in*) The delivery man disnae know there's umpteen women steyin here. Whit did he say? Flooers fur ye, hen? Ye open the door, expectin me an see a man. Didn't ye get a fricht?

(*confused, Beth nods agreement*)

SADIE: See? A helluva fricht. Widnae hear whit name he said. Look, your man disnae ken whaur ye are. Ye could be onywhere. It isnae easy tae fund oot this address. Carolanne's man hud the phone number fur a while before he phoned. He'll huv been scourin the area till he fund the right hoose.

AGNES: Right an all. Furst the phone call. Then the flooers. An if that hudnae worked…

SADIE: (*cutting in*) An anither thing. Carolanne's man aywis geid hur flooers efter he duffed her up. (*to Beth*) How often did your man gie you flooers?

(*Beth shakes her head. Upstairs, the baby shrieks*)

SADIE: There ye are then. (*tosses flowers onto the table*) Whit a fuss ower somedy else's flooers. Gaunae get up. I cannae staun seein a wummin oan her knees. An that wean's daen ma heid in.

(*as Beth goes for the baby's bottle, Gordon holds it out and Beth meets his eyes before accepting it. About to exit, Beth turns as if to speak. Sadie cuts her off*)

SADIE: Dinnae say ye're sorry. Sorry's no allowed in here.

(*Beth exits. Sadie leans on table. Agnes watches her*)

GORDON: Will I make tea?

SADIE: Put yer books away furst, will ye?

GORDON: (*hesitates, knowing something isn't right*) Mum?

SADIE: Just put yer books away.

GORDON: (*sighs*) Right.

(*Gordon takes his bag of school books and exits. Sadie looks at Agnes. The two women stare at each other*)

AGNES: Whit ur we gaunae dae?

(*Sadie turns, grabs the bouquet and beats the flowers to shreds against the table in a vicious, uncontrolled display or rage and fear. When her fury's exhausted, the floor covered in scraps of flowers, she puts her hands back on the table, back to Agnes, her head down*)

AGNES: Ye didnae like the flooers then?

SADIE: (*turns*) Whit are we gaunae dae, Agnes?

AGNES: Phone the helpline.

SADIE: They'll no move her noo till the morra. If they kin fund anither place even then.

AGNES: They kin get the polis tae step up their patrols.

SADIE: A caur drivin past wanst every couplae hours?

AGNES: Mibbe the'll be a worker free tae come an stey?

SADIE: Aye. An she'll be six feet twelve an armed tae the teeth. You ken thur isnae. Maggie's worked tae a frazzle as it is. I'm no daen it, Agnes. Sittin waitin fur somethin tae happen. No again. I'm goin, Agnes. Me an Gordon. First bus or train oot.

AGNES: Look. That man's no gaunnie risk gettin luftit by the polis. He's a doctur. He's goat his reputation tae think aboot. He'll be the persuasive type. Mair likely tae arrive wi a section order than spilin fur a fight.

SADIE: Sectioned? Ma man tried that yin – wi an axe. I huv tae go, Agnes.

AGNES: If onybody chaps the door, we kin act dumb. Dinnae answer it an they'll no git in.

SADIE: If onybody chaps onythin the night, I'll no hear cause I'll no *be* here.

AGNES: Whit aboot Beth?

SADIE: Whit aboot Beth? If he says jump, she'll jump.

AGNES: An if she cannae staun up tae him, wha will?

(*Sadie doesn't answer. Silence*)

AGNES: Look efter yer ain skin, then?

SADIE: Aye. There's no much ae it left hale but I'm kina attached tae whit is. (*more kindly*) Shut yersell in yer room, Agnes. Look the ither wey, same as awbody else. Battlin Bertha? It's just no me, pal.

AGNES: (*looking at mess of flowers*) Aye weel, at least ye gied the flooers a fricht.

Janet Paisley

scotland

she is a harsh mother,
arthritic with hills and crags
cut deeper than crow's feet.

her face is lined with ravines
her voice the roar of spume
on broken brown-toothed rock.

she passes boulders off as breasts,
belts her waist with an industrious past,
in her arms, she gathers firs

a grey and grizzled warrior, she is
bordered by ample hips, her tongue
a lash of thunderous voltage.

no season softens her, she drags
her children up on gorse and whin,
winters them without kindness.

she fires the hearth with ice or hail,
expects snow to pass for gentleness.
spring girdles her old in green.

if she holds you to her rugged breast
it is to pour the white-water scorn
of mountains on your head.

when she croons, she throws up seagulls.
sleeping, she drags a lumpen pillow
over the moon, punches out a few stars.

she'll turn your dreams to Scotch mist,
bone comb your hair with tugging wind
scrub your faces with rain.

in your mouth she lodges a language
no-one speaks, in your heart a stone.
but if you go from her

a wild song and dance will follow
to bind you forever son or daughter,
make you sick for home.

Janet Paisley

scotland

she's a haurd mither, sair
scartit wi braes an glens
oot-stravaigin ony craw's feet.

hur face glowers wi heuchs
hur vyce teems a burn in spate
ower broon-teeth jaggit scaurs.

she pits oan clinty craigs are briests,
belts hur waist wi forfochen industry,
in hur airms, she gethers firs.

aywis a thrawn, crabbit fechter, she's
boardered by fuller hips, flytin
fire-dairts wi thunnered micht.

nae season lichtens hur, she drags
hur bairns up oan kail an whin,
winters thaim athoot guidness.

she kennles the grate wi chitterin hail,
coups snaw tae shaw hoo saft she is.
spring claeths hur aulder in green.

if she coories ye in tae hur breist
it is tae skail a linn's white-watter
torrent o snash oantae yer heid.

liltin, she bokes up craikin maws.
sleepin, she bumphles a runkled pilla
ower the mune, batters oot twa three staurs.

she'll smoor yer dreams wi Scotch mist,
nit kaim yer hair wi chuggin wind,
slounge yer faces wi rain.

in yer mooth she staps a leid
naebody kens, in yer hert a stane.
but gang awa fae hur

a rantin sang an dance'll folley
tae reel ye in as son or dochter,
mak ye seik fur hame.

Alison Napier

I was born in Fife but moved to a village in the Highlands when I was ten, and although I have lived and worked in many other parts of Britain, each time I throw myself away I return like a boomerang to the far North. It is beauty and wild empty vistas and I love it – although it is frequently a little too cold.

In my twenties I studied sociology at Aberdeen University, drove minibuses full of women to Greenham Common, discovered politics and feminism and came out as a lesbian. I found Mary Daly and Adrienne Rich and Kate Millet (but not their Scottish counterparts) and the things I wrote then were letters and press releases, and stories and diaries, and a forty thousand-word manuscript about my experiences as a patient in a mental hospital when I was a teenager. All grist to the mill.

Ten years later I became a social worker, a job I now do part-time. Over the years my writing has appeared in, amongst others, *Riptide* (Two Ravens Press 2007), *New Internationalist*, *The Guardian* and *The Observer*. 'Stac Jenny' was a prize-winner in the Neil Gunn Writing Competition 2007 and I am very proud of her.

I live with my partner in Sutherland and I write two or three days a week, dashing from the house with a laptop and a flask of coffee to an elderly thirteen-foot caravan nearby, the rain stotting off the tin roof, buffeted with gales and storms.

My stories are about people at the margins, on the edge, who are puzzled by the contemporary rules of engagement. I write because life flings phrases and fables at me and I must obsessively record the everyday chaos and magic that is all around.

My first novel is nearing completion.

Alison Napier

Stac Jenny

My beautiful daughter is wearing blue today. Kingfisher and cornflower blue, a joyous and radiant wave-blue that reflects the cloudless skies as she flings the window open and announces, 'Another sunny day, Jennifer. Time to get up. We'll get out today, I think. Yes. Most certainly.' I am watching her from my bed, and thinking that she has adopted a curious manner of speech but that none the less I like it. It reflects the temporary formality of our relationship. Not many return after so long away and I am deeply grateful. 'Certainly,' I echo. 'We'll get out.'

We will get out and we will voyage to where the earth ends and the oceans begin. We will travel and trek on the ancient tracks that scar and score and criss and cross the land, with a bundle of clothes and hearty life-saving sustenance in my backpack, safe in my heavy leather coat which I wear over clumsily knitted layers of jumpers, one row plain one row purl, and shoes too big as if we had run away in the middle of playing dressing up in Mother's wardrobe, run away with squeals of laughter at the visions we made, a stiff white Courtelle cardigan over a floral print summer frock that reaches my feet, my heels slithering off the high cream strappy sandals, my toes jammed painfully in the points, swinging a fake crocodile handbag, inhaling the sweet pink smell of the powder puff, the compact, the secrets of motherhood, and the painted wound on the lips, stuck together lips, all made up. What a get-up. Get up. Up and get out. Yes, we will certainly get out.

◆ ◆ ◆

And this is my home, he said. This here is my home. Blue door and blue window frames set deep in uneven flaking whitewashed walls, moorland behind and sandy machair meadow in front, all held in check by mossy tumbledown drystone walls, all guarded by the rowan who never leaves her post. You should carry me over the threshold I laughed but he was already inside, inside the porch and fumbling, fumbling with the key in the inside door. Fumbling inside. I followed him in and put down my cardboard suitcase in the hall, at the foot of the steep wooden stairs. I followed him into the kitchen and watched him as he looked around, looking for something, his life perhaps. This had been his uncle's house, he had explained to me. It's mine now. Well, ours, I suppose.

The kitchen was cramped and dim, the window frame peeling faded denim blue paint, with a dusty range against the end wall and a chipped, deep double sink in the corner. There was a bible, waiting, on the yellow Formica-covered table and a tall prim pale-green dresser with sliding glass doors that revealed cups and saucers, side plates and dinner plates, plain and patternless, and there was a church pew, piously uncushioned, the length of the wall beneath the window. Oak, polished with the posteriors of penitent parishioners.

I prepared a banquet. 'Our wedding feast,' I announced proudly. I stewed the rabbit that a neighbour had delivered, who had refused to come in, flushed with embarrassment. I boiled it up with onions and with parsley from the garden, I peeled potatoes and tossed them in too, carefree, along with turnip and parsnips and carrots, and earthy shavings and peelings from my vegetables piled up on the chopping board beneath the knife, a hillside of golden bracken in the evening sunlight, a tangle of seaweed ribbons and tangerine twine on the shingle. Our dinner took shape on the range that I had coaxed into life, twists of paper, twigs and kindling, a splash of paraffin, and dry peats.

We sat side by side on the pew and ate in silence. I did not mind. I was contented with the meal and I could hear the gulls and the waves and the creaking of the old walls. Then he went outside and all I could see through the door was the bright orange glow and fade of a star as he inhaled his cigarette. Later, upstairs between thin joyless sheets, a different shocked silence crashed round the room. I listened carefully. I could hear the future. I started to hum a lament that no one could hear but me.

One morning he left. He said nothing and he took nothing. No, that is perhaps not altogether true. He tore down the brilliant blue of the sky and bundled up the breakers on the beach and shoved them roughly into his satchel and I searched in vain for the proud weathers and the winds. He ripped the rippling white sands from the shores and left only the jagged ragged rock pools, and from these he stole the mermaids' purses and the tiny cowry shells, *cypraea moneta*, the currency for our future.

And some months later I wrapped my possessions in a scarlet blanket and we set off.

I knew what they were saying about me as I sang my way up the coast and then back down again. Neither up nor down. And for me some scarlet ribbons. They were saying that I was mad, that my mind was lost and abandoned, that something crucial that was attaching it to who knows what had become un-hinged. That I was de-ranged. And yet what possible harm can I do, I thought, because the greatest danger lies in action, and be assured there is no action left in this cracked and weary shell.

Discard after use. Not for resale. Unfit for human consumption. Consume within three days. There is a ship in Spanish Harlem. Pay no heed, attention all shipping, take no notice, take nothing at all, I felt the knife in my hand, I am a pillar of salt carved to curves by the waves that suck my smooth outlines, gentle teasing licks in a Force Two, crests have a glassy appearance and do not break, and by my Storm Force, untamed heaving crests of waves heavy and shock like, visibility significantly affected. I change shape according to the weather, I am stac Jenny. Approach me if you dare.

The bundle used to cry, a fierce wail that stunned and stopped my fractured heart and wrenched lumps of rage from under my thin shirt and hurled them into the sea. The bundle used up all the life I had, and that I would have, and absorbed the love and the longing into her weak blotting-paper frame but it was not enough. The bundle was taken from me and I know I put up a fair fight. I screeched and screamed and hurled my rages at everyone who dared come near; the world was astonished at my strength. They came too close so I fled, a nightmare flight in ill-fitting shoes and a heavy leather coat, clutching my bundle, clanking robotically in my useless suit of armour, stumbling on the sheep-shorn machair arms legs heart all broken up and breaking down as I head for the waves, and nurses in blue and doctors in white, disguised as breakers, just smiled or so it seemed, and took my sunshine away. You'll never know, dear. I searched, I did, I searched in vain. Sorry. I do recall an unseemly scuffle.

But scuffles come and scuffles go, come and go, as tides rise and fall. Soon the echoes in my hollow spaces diminished and I returned to the address I had given as home to the home-breakers. The diminishing returns of stac Jenny, I explained to my neighbour who still brought me rabbits, only smaller now. He smiled, baffled but brave, coming and going, as if it mattered.

I have chopped the pew up into kindling. Now I sit alone on a deckchair. I have reclaimed the Best Room, the one at the front where I was not allowed to go, and I sit on a deckchair because the armchairs have mice living in them. And no mouse ever lived in a deckchair. This much I know.

I have a knife and I sit on my deckchair and I whittle and carve, shavings scattered round my feet. So far I have made thirty-seven tent pegs, each one carved into a nine-inch tall thin doctor or a nine-inch tall thin nurse. I hammer them into the ground around my house to make sure they are working. They are working. And I have carved a spurtle with a mermaid figure head, her hair flies out behind her and her chin is raised in defiance and her eyes stare blankly out across the boiling seas in my porridge pan every morning.

I have walked the moors, the mad moines, those wide open spaces that share their skies with deserts and steppes, with prairies and plains; I have walked and walked towards all the horizons with my wheelbarrow pram and crept down into deep dark ditches and clawed at the buried bleached branches poking out of the peat, the fossilised timber that waits for me in the trenches. My nails bleed and my feet are rotting and sinking but I drag the limbs out and push them home, whispering and singing. Then

I wash each one in a tin bath-tub in the kitchen, with hand-hot water, a clean rag and scented soap, tenderly and lovingly, cotton-buds into all its secret private places, I soothe the bruises and I ease the twists and gnarls, I wrap it in a towel-blanket and hold it close to me, rocking it to sleep, humming a lament. Once they are stilled I lay them to rest outside by the sentry rowan and they are warmed by the summer suns and cleansed by the winter winds. When the weather allows I take my deckchair outside and I sit and polish them with the finest sandpaper and massage them with linseed oils. In this way I know they will stay with me forever and indeed they do.

Immaculate gleaming camper vans, shimmering like Taj Mahals, smug in their self-containment, come and park in the field that belongs to the rabbit-man. The grass is clipped closer than a carpet. *All Campers Welcome* his sign proclaims, and I can see the row of bungalows on wheels, parked side by side in a perfect recreation of a suburban street. A brave few wander across the dunes as far as here, plucky little Lawrences of Arabia, and stare into my garden. I offer them a few cabbage leaves but they decline, profuse in their thanks. This is not what they want. Perhaps they do not cook. I cook every day, soup from vegetable-scraps and rabbit-bones, scones, the dough soft as an infant's breath, and hearty life-saving stews with beans and peas and roots, and strands of seaweed, salty iodine memories for seasoning. I grow cabbages, carrots and kale in the dry Sahara soil, and I protect the shoots with flotsam and jetsam, with upturned lobster-pots and bundles of runaway nets and plastic containers from foreign fishing fleets, blow-ins, and corks and faded floats hang from the rowan to ward off evil spirits and so far this has proved successful. Evil spirits are warded off and the kale stands tall.

The brave who venture here admire the polished artefacts in many languages, a few of which I understand. Mad amounts of money are offered for the jewels in my crown, for my fossil family, the trench people, and I say *No* in many languages. I offer up the tent pegs instead, traditional ethnic folk-carvings, local totems, I confirm. 'Tent-pegs!' they laugh, delighted, and so in this way my captors and robbers are scattered about the globe, to be perched on mantelpieces, or accidentally burned, or hidden in attics, or displayed behind glass with other precious artefacts, while I receive a modest income for life's essentials. Who would have thought it. *Cypraea moneta.*

◈ ◈ ◈

Yes yes yes yes yes. Yes. Certainly. Today we are going to the café, the one at the campsite. Blue, blue, a kind of blue, nobody knows the trouble I'm in, this gnarled and twisted limb is rotting on the vine, once bitten three O'Leary, they will wash me in hand-hot water with a tenderness to die for, and soothe creams and oils into the cracked leather because I'm worth it and polish me until all the ragged jagged edges are smooth again. They will use me for their dressing-up game and disguise me as someone's mother. And then and only then will I be placed, this time surely, on the long trolley barrow-pram and wheeled out to the garden to join the others, eased into a deckchair, to season and weather under the protection of the rowan, to wait and watch and wait and watch, with this kind foreign stranger, who pretends so faultlessly, in kingfisher breaker blue.

Laureen Johnson

I was born in 1949 and grew up on a croft in Shetland, in a lively, close-knit community. After university and work on the Scottish mainland, I returned to my home village to get married, and have lived there ever since. I've written plays, poems, and short stories, a local history book, and a short novel, *Shetland Black* (2002). *Treeds,* a pamphlet of my poems, was published in 2007. My work appears in the *New Shetlander* magazine, and has appeared in various Scottish publications.

Women play an important role in Shetland society. The islands' seafaring past, where men were often absent for long periods of time, meant that Shetland women developed a tradition of independence. Their work on the land, and their skills in knitting, were often vital to the economic survival of families and communities. The late twentieth century brought Shetland prosperity, an influx of population, and many changes in lifestyle. Job opportunities increased for women, and these included a great many more jobs at higher education level. Previously, Shetland university students wishing to return home more or less had to become teachers.

I have never considered gender as an issue in writing in Shetland. The biggest issue for a dialect speaker like me is the choice of which voice to use. Educated to write in English, I often write most happily the way I speak. But it's not really a conscious decision, more of an instinct.

Grey

Nooadays, it's a choice we hae,
whan ta go grey.
So it's a kind o statement.
What does it say?

'Weel, yon's yon'?
'Don't care, it's just hair'??

What signifees grey
in wir day?
Da aald, wise head?
Experience? Maturity? – Yea!
(A sweeter tune fae
an aalder fiddle, dey say!)
Grey ... da fashion shedd?

Grey, nedder black nor white,
  aye in atween, hesitatin.
Grey laek schöl skirts
grey laek battleships
grey laek steel
grey laek washing machine misanters
grey laek mist
  faaldin aboot you
dowed grey,
dirty-white grey,
wishen-oot grey,
faded an grey...

Ach, it's only a shedd on a shedd caird!

Yes, caa'd 'Pearl' or 'Silver',
'Charcoal' or 'Dove' or 'Winter Moon'
or 'Evening Silk' or onything idder
– onything idder as *grey*!

Maybe I'll wait till da time is right
an just go
white.

What signifees grey? *– what does grey mean?*
Shedd *– shade;* ***misanters*** *– accidents;* ***dowed*** *– faded;*
wishen-oot *– washed-out*

Laureen Johnson

Elvis's jacket

Claes ta her
wis dat important –
mair as a covering,
mair as a daecency,
mair as comfort, even.
Claes wis laek
a message-board,
a flag, an advertisement.
Claes gae impressions,
sent signals,
set moods an standards.
She ignored
my comments aboot pigs in pokes,
an shallowness, an 'tak me as dey fin me'.

Da idder night I sat an watched a programme
aboot Elvis's jacket,
his G.I. jacket, twartree sizes peerie
for him at peyed da fortune juist ta have it
an tak it oot sometimes an look, an touch it,
an feel delight.
An I began ta tink
o braid an badges laid by in a box,
a costume bowt wi money fae da guttin
a life ago,
an idder things mair near ta me:

a wedding veil,
a peerie cuddly sleepy-suit
an haand-made laecy cardigans I hardly wöre.

It's only claes, I say,
an say again, but never fire it oot!
Ony mair as wid da millionaire
wi Elvis's jacket.

---

twartree *– several;* ***costume*** *– woman's suit*

Joy Hendry

Joy Hendry was born in Perth, 1953. She attended Edinburgh University from 1970 to 1976, studying English and philosophy, and also joint-edited the then-nascent *Chapman* magazine, becoming its sole editor in 1976. She taught English for seven years before becoming a full-time editor, writer, lecturer and broadcaster in 1984. She lectured in drama for Queen Margaret College and in periodical journalism for Napier College, Edinburgh (2000–04).

Stimulated by scant publishing opportunities, particularly for poets, she started The Chapman New Writing Series, which has published authors such as Magi Gibson, Janet Paisley, George Gunn, Tom Scott, Lydia Robb, Ian Abbot and Colin Mackay. She has also edited volumes of critical essays on Sorley MacLean and Norman MacCaig (with Raymond Ross), and written and edited various other works too numerous to mention.

Her journalistic career includes theatre criticism for *The Scotsman*, *The Herald*, *The Guardian* and extensively on Radios 3, 4 and Radio Scotland, and she contributes regularly to radio (and occasionally TV) discussion programmes. From 1988–1997 she was the radio critic of *The Scotsman*. She has written poetry all her life, but also drama, notably her play about William Soutar, *Gang Doun wi a Sang* (Perth, 1990). She also wrote a schools' play about Soutar, and a full-length radio play, *The Wa' at the Warld's End* was broadcast on Radio 3 in 1993. In addition, partly through the magazine, and partly as an individual, she has worked as a general cultural *agent provocateur*, stimulating change and progress in artistic fields: literature, theatre etc. She also has interfered in constitutional and 'political' matters, helping to produce *A Claim of Right for Scotland* which led ultimately to the creation of the Scottish Parliament in 1997, and Scots language, educational policy, and the publishing scene in Scotland. She was awarded an Honorary D Litt from the University of Edinburgh in 2005 for her services to Scotland and Scottish literature.

While Chronic Fatigue has limited her activities over the last ten years or so, she continues to edit the magazine and write, and looks forward gradually to resuming her public role as meddler, mover and stirrer.

Joy Hendry

The Invisible Women of Scotland – coming into their own at last

My title is inspired by the late Alexander Scott, poet, academic, a prickly, contermashious character to whom we owe a great deal culturally. He was also responsible for starting and perpetuating a great deal of trouble – literary feuds and the like. It was 1980; we were at a reception at the house of, I think, Joan Lingard. The penny had finally dropped for me that the Scottish literary world was virtually a woman-free zone and that something had to be done about it. Look at Charles King's first schools anthology, *Twelve Modern Scottish Poets* (Hodder & Stoughton, 1971) – no women at all! Mentions in the various Histories of Scottish Literature were confined mostly to derisory, snide remarks about the third-rate, homespun nature of their work. The Scottish malerati had grudgingly accepted Helen B Cruickshank – a virgin, and trapped in the role of caring for her mother – as someone due some credit for her role in creating and running Scottish PEN – but her poetry – well...

So I had asked Alex, the only Professor of Scottish Literature with the only Chair of Scottish Literature, for his thoughts on Scottish women poets. 'Scottish women poets,' he replied, aghast. 'You mean there *are* any?' He wasn't just being provocative.

The gradual dropping of the penny had stimulated me to look around and realise that *nothing* had been done to note and appreciate the contribution of women to Scottish poetry, and, looking further, there was precious little too about women in fiction, music, the visual arts – you name it, it wasn't there! I have to confess that when I started publishing my own poetry in the early 1970s, I did so under the name 'J M Hendry' because I wanted to see if anyone could identify me as a woman – and if they didn't, then that was a sign that the poems were 'strong'. Dearie me! It worked: everyone assumed that JMH was a man. After a couple of years, I began to think there was something wrong with this.

After a few years of gradual enlightenment, and accumulating outrage at the neglect of women, I set about compiling a special issue of *Chapman* which eventually appeared in August 1980 under the title: *Woven by Women* – devoted to celebrating the achievement of Scottish women in the arts and culture – against all the odds. I think the flame to the fuse came the previous year when I was asked to give a talk on 'Women in Poetry' to the Haddington Lamp of Lothian, which made me realise my chronic ignorance. So I whopped it to them – Anna Akhmatova, Marina Tsvetaeva – mainly European women. They were more than a little overwhelmed by what they got, and never asked me back! But when I looked at what I'd written, I realised that there were no Scottish women mentioned in despatches. Why not?

Accepted on the 'scene' at the time was Liz Lochhead, with Valerie Gillies and Tessa Ransford there more or less on sufferance. The success of Lochhead was put down to the 'poppy' and 'populist' nature of *Memo for Spring*, which had sold out several times. And the huge success of Flora Garry in Aberdeen and environs was attributed to local enthusiams. Maurice Lindsay had put down VJ, MA and HMC as 'shrinking Violets and home-made Marions' in his *History of Scottish Literature* (Robert Hale, 1977) – even Robert Crawford and W N Herbert got silly fun with jibes in their poem 'Cleggs' which counselled: 'dinnae try tae bile yir heid/ In Biolet Jacob's auld kail poat' (*Sterts & Stobies*, Obog Books, 1985).

It was an accepted principle that women couldn't write poetry – verse, maybe; poetry, 'no'. The relatively social and domestic genre of fiction they were allowed – distaff stuff, drama was OK – just – but the holy grail of poetry was something they shouldn't even bother to aspire to. Their role in poetry, if anything, was as Muse figure – as some mooning goddess, or romantically, as a backstage dictator of the imagination, a handmaiden who might, if she played her cards right, be permitted to wash poets' dirty feet. As Muse figure, she was celebrated in poems by the likes of Tom Scott; Sorley MacLean had several mysterious women, mainly unrequited loves, occupying that position. And there was, in more real terms, the tragic figure of Stella Cartwright – personal Muse to probably half the twelve men in *Twelve Modern Scottish Poets* and others forbye.

Even Kathleen Raine, who professed herself Scottish by virtue of her Scottish mother, from whom she had inherited, learned and developed her sense of music, song and poetry – and, most importantly, her febrile imagination – repudiated women's capabilities in the realm of poetry. I argued bitterly with her to the end about this, provoking the haughty, patrician side of her to dismiss me as a rabid Feminist (which I think I've only been for a few angry seconds here and there). 'Joy's a wonderful woman. What a pity she's a Feminist,' she said to my niece, who was researching Willa Muir for a PhD. But, fundamentally, we were sisters in literature despite the age difference. We were also sister editors. I remember getting a Christmas card from her, with the gleeful addition to the customary Season's Greeting: 'I'm an editor too now.' That was in 1980, when I was in touch with her about contributing to *Woven by Women*. And there she was, starting out on the gargantuan task of creating and editing a very substantial magazine indeed, *Temenos*, at the age of seventy-two.

Kathleen was an inspiration, as was Naomi Mitchison, who had 'come out' as a poet too, on top of all her other gifts and achievements, in *The Cleansing of the Knife* (Canongate, 1979). Naomi was always coy about her poetry, buying into the prevailing mythology that women could never really be poets. I was privileged to get to know her quite well, amongst other things making a radio tribute and doing a major radio interview with her on the occasion of her 90th birthday – but she would never be cajoled into regarding herself as a poet – just about everything else under the sun, and of course she was a great champion of women's rights, sexual freedom – and so on, but, poetry – well ... it's the men who do that.

Another important female inspiration for me was Jessie Kesson. Again, it was the creation of *Woven by Women* which brought me in touch with her. I reviewed her novel *The White Bird Passes*, which had recently been re-issued by Paul Harris Publishing. The review had just a bit of the *de haut en bas* about it. I was irritated by claims in the introduction by Cuthbert Graham of the *Aberdeen Press and Journal*, that she was on a par with Lewis Grassic Gibbon's *A Scots Quair* in her achievement. Clearly that claim was a nonsense – the intellectual and cultural range, the sheer bigness of scope and vision just isn't there in *A White Bird*. I said so. To my surprise, I got a long and appreciative letter from Jessie, saying that I was quite right, agreeing that invidious comparisons did her no favours at all. Our friendship lasted until her death in 1994. She regularly travelled from her London home to Scotland to participate in events I was organising – and we made a memorable trip round her childhood haunts, Elgin, Inverness, the Orphanage at Skene, the Black Isle, setting for *Another Time Another Place* and The Glens of Foundry, setting for *A Glitter of Mica* – and Abriachan, where she was orphaned out after a nervous breakdown and met her husband, Johnnie. The expedition was written up for *The Scots Magazine*.

The trip forced her to relive many painful experiences, which made her difficult to deal with. But we got there in the end, still friends despite some quite vicious spats. I could fill the rest of this essay with anecdotes about her carryings-on. But, it was a wonderful experience. She was very brave, aged about seventy-three, to undertake it at all, especially considering that the strictures of the *Scots Magazine* expenses allowance forced us to do all this in three days. Jessie, too, fought very shy of seeing herself as a poet. I believe strongly that had it not been for this pernicious 'perception' about women and poetry, shared by women themselves, that all these women could and would have achieved much more in this field. This mental, internal 'ceiling', a kind of inhibiting self-censorship, is the more restricting of all.

Other women also helped with my literary and gender re-education: Wendy Wood, Valda Grieve (wife of Hugh MacDiarmid), and learning more about Willa Muir, Alice V Stuart, Joan Ure, Bessie J MacArthur – and of course The Singing Birds of Angus, Jacob, Cruickshank and Angus. (I once did a presentation of their work for Angus Libraries, and one man came along thinking he was getting a talk about canaries!) I set myself to read as much by and about them as I could, and, quite apart from *Woven by Women*, did as much as I could to draw their worth to the attention of other people. I was lucky indeed in my poetic grandmothers.

Editing that issue was an inspiring, humiliating and life-changing experience. At a conference in Salzburg on British literature, run by the enterprising Institüt für Anglistik & Amerikanist of Salzburg University in 1996, Patricia Oxley, editor of *Acumen*, described editing a magazine as 'educating oneself in public'. How true. While my views on women, and women in literature, poetry in particular, had been changing, it took the process of assembling the issue to make the real difference. I was humbled, yes, humiliated, at my own blinkered stupidity and ignorance. I was hugely grateful for the responses from the women I was working with, including the younger generation of Liz Lochhead, Valerie Gillies, Tessa Ransford, my American professor friend Nancy Gish who was researching Hugh MacDiarmid – and many others. How different the process was from a 'normal' issue of *Chapman*. Looking back at early issues, the magazine's record wasn't much better than Charlie King's in that first anthology – only a couple of women, if that, in any one issue! The policy emerged, quite spontaneously, that the creation of this issue was a team effort, and the extent of cooperation, encouragement and enthusiasm from all the contributors (including the men writing about women – Alasdair Gray on Joan Ure, John Purser on Scottish Women Composers, George N Scott on Willa Muir, Ronald Stevenson on Helen B) was extraordinary. Much of the same spirit was still discernible in 1993, when we tried to repeat the performance with *The Women's Forum*, issues 74–77 – but you can't do the same thing twice, and it didn't make anything like the same impact. My assistant, Peter Cudmore, remarked ruefully when we returned to 'normal': 'Oh dear. It's back to dealing with men and male egos!'

But *Woven by Women* did make a huge impact, provoking considerable debate in *The Scotsman* and *The Glasgow Herald* and elsewhere. All manner of other things started to happen, anthologies such as Cathleen Kerrigan's, critical articles, PhDs… I was asked to write a chapter on Scottish women poets for Cairns Craig's *History of Scottish Literature*. I was, admittedly, proud of what I'd started off, but also hurt by how little of it involved me. One of the 'problems' I've always faced as an editor is that I work outside the world of academe, with only a poor Second Class Honours Degree in Mental Philosophy. I 'wasted' much of my undergraduate years on *Chapman* and the literary world, and, most of all, selling it and other magazines in pubs and round universities, which both enabled the magazine to exist and brought in much-needed money. Thereby hang many other tales! While *Woven by Women* may have lit the fuse, its editor lacked proper educational and academic credentials, and so, ultimately, intellectual and social authority, and I got sidelined thereafter, about which I remain a little bitter. The same has happened in other fields, such as Scots Language, in which I've played a key role at times. Ah well.

It's worth noting too that when I became joint editor of *Chapman* in 1972 and then sole editor in 1976, I was, to my knowledge, the first woman editor ever in Scotland. Some of the established poets of the time regarded me with dismissive disdain, and the Scottish Arts Council deprived me of my grant after only two issues of sole editorship. But I got nothing but encouragement from the likes of Norman MacCaig, Sorley MacLean, Iain Crichton Smith, Tom Scott, Robert Garioch, Alasdair Gray, George Mackay Brown and others, all of whom rallied round to protest against SAC's decision and supported me by contributing to the magazine themselves. None of them were entirely New Age Men, or unsullied by male chauvinism – as one might expect of that generation – but my gender or tender age didn't matter so long as I was doing work they thought worthwhile. I was privileged to become quite close friends with most of them.

I still had more thinking to do, as I hinted in my words earlier on the review of *The White Bird Passes*. I began to question the literary criteria I had absorbed from the ether and 'education'. There was something not quite right. It was clear that women do think and operate generally in a different way from men, and it would seem to follow that when it came to the writing of poetry, and literature generally, that they would bring a different set of tools and precepts to the job. Furthermore, the jobs they choose to tackle might be different from those undertaken by male writers. Why criticise an egg for not being an apple, and who is to say which is better? Two things: firstly, women writers – the fact is that they are not trying to do the same job, and they are using different tools differently, and have different priorities. To express this in something of a cliché, emotional, personal and social matters are a higher priority for women, and their most important tools are intuition, instinct and feeling, whereas men tend to regard objectivity and intellect as of key importance. Men have made all the rules in poetry especially, so naturally, judged by those rules, women seem to fail. So the pecking order, the critical principles had to be questioned and re-analysed: Why, for example, is 'intellect' 'better' than any of the other human attributes?

As history has now shown, some of these rules and critical principles *were* just plain wrong, and a plethora of additional ones are required to make judgements about women's writing. The explosion in writing by women over the last thirty years has blown the whole scene apart, adding entirely new dimensions and freeing things up in a way inconceivable thirty years ago. It's been a liberation for the men, too. So what was right about my response to Jessie's generous acceptance of my criticism was that, gratified though I was, I was left scratching my head, thinking that something wasn't quite right. The fact is that in its own and any terms, *The White Bird Passes* is a truly remarkable work of fiction. No man could ever have written it, nor take the stylistic liberties Jessie took. It operates in a different world, and on a different scale altogether. In *The White Bird*, Jessie is trying for the most intimate of stories; she is a miniaturist, not a cultural metaphysician. Similarly Violet Jacob's *The Wild Geese* is perfect in its own terms, and has the courage to allow genuine emotion to fly as high as the geese themselves. Ditto Helen B's *Shy Geordi*. I know of few who can listen to Jim Reid's superb rendering of these as songs and remain dry-eyed. Under the old rules, this is a weakness; we have learned now that it is no such thing.

Secondly, Scotland: in 1983 or thereabouts I took part in a Women's Writing Conference in Edinburgh delivering a lecture called 'The Double Knot in the Peeny', later published by Hutchison in the volume *In Other Words* (1987). My theory ran roughly thus: that Scottish women are at a two-fold disadvantage, because they are at two removes from the handles of power – and this operated (I gladly use the past tense) most importantly in politics, and in the arts, especially music and of course literature. It operated in everything else as well, even the promotion and distribution of tins of shortbread. Women, being subservient to and dependent on men, certainly socially if not on a personal level, had also to cope with the psychological impact of the loss of social independence in 1603 and political independence in

1707 – an experience similar to castration. Putting it differently, it was like being tied to a tied animal.

Looking back on it all now, I breathe a profound sigh of relief and gratitude. We have gone through the stage of tokenism, and the process of overcompensation. I remember pointing out to a respectable literary gent who was inviting me to join a discussion panel that there were no other women involved. He replied: 'Oh, we asked Liz Lochhead, but she couldn't come. We thought we *had* to ask one woman, so we're asking you!' Thanks! But I think we've finally reached the stage where you are expected and allowed to get where you want to get to or not, more or less on your own merits (although not *all* battles are won). We can stop being too self-conscious about what it means to *be* a woman writer (which used to send Jessie into a fury) and just get on with *doing* it. Same goes for being Scottish – we had to go through a pretty intense process of self-examination, navel gazing, protesting about imbalances, pondering about identity – all that stuff. *Hasta la vista*! In a healthy society, the individual can simply *be*, wearing both gender and identity like an invisible, many-coloured cloak. At one point I was positively stigmatised and ridiculed for my protestations about the imbalances of gender, and the need for political autonomy and promotion of things Scottish, including Scots and Gaelic. I was dubbed 'an East Coastie Cult-Nat' and enjoyed various other such compliments.

I was impelled to all this by an acute sense of injustice, driven by a force I cannot explain. My protestant, pantheistic agnosticism never lets me off the hook. It is good to think that some of the pain and labour of years has borne a little juicy fruit. Scotland as a whole is now very much on the map, and women in Scotland in particular are more than ubiquitously visible as a highly potent part of the human race, willing and eager to contribute what only they can.

On a personal level, people may find it hard to believe that I've always operated out of a chronic lack of self-confidence, that with everything I do, even writing this essay, I must first overcome an enormous lack of self-belief. That *does* come from my upbringing, and I wrote extensively about this in my essay in *The Spirit of Scotland* (The Saltire Society, 2005). While from an early age (as long ago as I can remember) I vehemently rejected all notions that my sex should debar me from anything whatsoever, I *was* nonetheless profoundly affected by the prejudices endemic at the time. Being a huge child (5ft 10 by age ten), and strong-faced, my femininity and sexuality were rubbished by all and sundry, including my family. My father once told me, emphatically, that I would never have a good figure because I was too tall, and that I would inevitably end up like my Auntie Jessie, twenty stones and virtually immobile. Even to this day yobbos will shout after me in the street: 'Is that a laddie or a lassie' – or, nowadays 'a man or a wumman'. Probably most damaging of all has been the quite mistaken notion that the most important thing in life is to be loved. Being 'a strong woman' means, amongst other things, that you attract people who want to first of all take advantage of your strength, and then, having done that, to try to destroy that positive strength, to rid themselves of some threat that you seem to pose. Well, I'm still here, if at times in the last ten or so years, battling chronic fatigue, it has been only just, by the tips of my fingernails.

I am haunted by the end of Norman MacCaig's poem, *A Man in Assynt*, which speculates that maybe now there can be 'new generations replenishing the land/ with its richest of riches and coming, at last,/ into their own again', having cleaved the rocks and debris once and for all. Perhaps, I've reached the place where I too can come at last into my self, maybe for the first time.

Survivor

Me – naethin!
Widnae think it, luikin at me –
big wumman, hair'n'that,
stridin oot fit tae demolish a fitbaa team
worth millions.

Worth naethin, me.
Widnae get a tenner staunin at the street corner,
high heels, fishnets,
buttocks oot ma short-skirt arse
'n ma thumb oot.

Surprise, surpise.
Nae takers.

Whit'ye dae?
Hame an the voddy.
Plank yersel oot.

Mornin!
Mooth like the bottom of a budgie's cage!
Wretching fit tae burst.
Ma man's shoutin:
didnae get his hole, or his drink
'cos naebdy bought me!
At least a day's gone by.
Him staggerin aboot the kitchen,

pals screamin an lauchin
then aff tae bed,
pishin in his slippers
3 am!
Again!

Dis he think I dinnae ken?
Is ma nose cut aff?

Mornin, an there's pools in the carpet,
crap on the lino –
an the guff's enough
tae turn ye back tae the voddy.

Sex: ye're jokin!
Atween hangovers and 'seshs'
he's no worth a caa –
morning or night.
Gin ye stuffed a bottle up his
'thingummy',
naething culd stand.
Bairns is howlin,
tryin tae get aff tae schuill
but I cannae muve.
They ken the score:
Ah'm lucky no tae be black an blue
tae greet – an greet at
the rosy dawn.
Ah want thaim oot o this.

No anither day!

Ay, juist the same,
an aye the same.
Ye drag yersel up, arse first
so's no tae faa oot the bed –
swing yer legs thon wey.

Feet on the flair.
That's it!
A wee success!

Man's oot.
In the pub, for shair.
"Rest And Be Thankful".

Ootside sun's oot,
warm, blastin,
fowk stravaig, easy, lauchin,
in shorts, sandals –
Ah hate thaim!

The drouth in my thrapple
an the scaith in ma wame
maks a desert o the green leaves;
the flooers is ashen grey.

Ach weill. Fill the kettle.

Tomorrow's another day.

Joy Hendry

Mrs MacGrundy

(for my Auntie Jessie, Willa Muir
and the Bingo Women of Portobello/ Craigmillar)

See me –
Ah'm invincible!
When ah walk doon the street
aabody stares,
thir moos drap aipen,
they step intae the gutter
tae let me pass.
Thir's ainly room on this pavement
for yin o us
an Ah ken which wan
it's gonnae be.
See me –
Ah'm invincible.

Been on yin o thae diets
for twenty year –
nivir loast a pund yet
Gied up peanuts, cream cakes
swapped the pints o heavy
for a nip an a Carlsbeg Special –
but a wumman's goat ae huv
her fish suppers noo'n again.
See me –
Ah'm invincible.

See ma man,
smelly wee runt.
Tried tae pull a fast one
hav'n it away
wi the wumman next door.
Ah fix'd him!
Picked him up by the troosers
'n drapped him doon the sterr well
– her an aa.
'N when he came tae get me
Ah dunked his heid in the lavvy
See ma man –
he's a jelly.

See me –
Ah'm really a saftie.
'Mean Ah waanted people tae luve me, like,
waanted tae luik efter thaim
buy them Mars bars 'n Easter eggs. –
But Ah got that mony kicks in the teeth
Ah hud falsers afore Ah went tae the schule
beat'n up – regular
abused – the usual bit.
So Ah said: Fuck this
fur a gemm o sodjers.
But, see me –
Ah'm really a saftie.

See me –
Ah'm invincible
Ah'm tolerant, like.
'Mean I juist cannae staun onyb'dy
that contradicts mi.
An if ye dae Ah warn ye
Wha daur meddle wi me?
Naeb'dy 'xceptin Jesus Christ –
or King Kong.
See me.
Ah'm invincible.

Mandy Haggith

I was born in Northumberland but have spent most of my adult life in Scotland. As a Geordie, Scotland always seemed a more welcoming place than England, with Edinburgh a closer and more familiar capital city than faraway London. The annual call of the festival was enough to make me a regular visitor and I moved there in 1987 to do a masters degree at Edinburgh University. I've been this side of the border ever since, making my way north to the Highlands after I fell in love with a crofter.

When I am not writing I am mostly trying to save the world's forests, although the overlap between writing and activism is increasing, so I am often not sure which I'm doing. At the moment I am particularly focused on the excesses of the paper industry. Forestry is a male-dominated field, as was my previous career in computing. The literary universe seems very different, with women in the ascendant.

Being a writer in Scotland feels like being part of a remarkably friendly and supportive community, and one in which many of the contemporary leaders are women. I'm thinking of both poets (Liz Lochhead, Kathleen Jamie, to name but two) and novelists (Janice Galloway, Margaret Elphinstone), but also of those who run literary institutions like the Scottish Poetry Library, the Edinburgh Book Festival and magazines like *Chapman, Poetry Scotland* and *Northwords Now*. Perhaps in a previous era this was a male-dominated world, with whisky-fuelled Scots machismo brandished in smoky bars, but I seem to have walked in after the revolution. To the women who struggled to carve out this space, thank you.

Being Forty

It's not suckling.
Not feeding a baby on milk from within.
Not having breasts round with nourishment.

It's not having a life growing inside.
Not growing fat in loose dresses.
Not watching the belly swell.

It's not feeling the pain of labour.
Not having contractions, pushing, breathing until the
waters break.
Not reassured by a midwife.

It's not smelling the newborn, not hearing its cry.
Not smiling at the first yawn, at little fists.
Not looking into newly opened eyes.

It's not one of these things.
None of them.
None of them at all.

Paper Daughter

Gestate inside a private writing room
the person of your choosing. Cut her gently
out of paper, follow dotted lines,
bend along the creases saying “fold here”.

Snip scissors, careful not to crop off curls,
draw in the face you want to set free
smiling, frowning, choose whose eyes
will weep and watch and see.

Press out some clothes to dress her up in,
cardboard jeans and shirt or tissue dress,
hook their paper tabs around her shoulders
sure not to crush their smooth white newness.

Prop her on her stand beside a candle flame.
Feel inside you rustling cells embroider.
Let them replicate as you create
then burn your paper daughter.

Mandy Haggith

carry carry life finish

alone it's hard to hoist
a back-basket full of seaweed

to straighten knees and lift
the woven willow shoulder-borne

the strap across the forehead
padded with soft remnants of a toy

its comforting tug across the brow
with every footfall

heavier than normal
stepping back in time

remembering a Nepali friend
resting with a doko full of dung

sighing *carry carry life finish*
with a smiling wobble of the head

now the slow heave up the hill
the awkward manoeuvre at the gate

hands grasping the knotted rope
grasping the hands of other women

in other countries
in other millennia

marching alone in solidarity
with all the other creel-bearers

singing *carry carry life finish*
though clearly life goes on

Lesley McDowell

I was born in Glasgow in 1967, and in spite of short residencies in Antwerp and St Andrews, this is the city I've chosen to stay in for most of the last forty years. I remember, at age twenty, thinking that I could live anywhere – the only problem was, there were so many amazing places to choose from. But friends and family pulled me back

I studied feminist theory as part of my PhD on James Joyce back in the early '90s – it was Anglo-American literary feminism that first attracted me, and then I got hooked by the French feminists: Cixous, Irigaray and Kristeva. Both groups were interested in how women wrote, what their concerns were, how they played with language and so on. I loved the idea then that women wrote differently from men, whether for biological, social or political reasons.

Now, I think the demarcations are far more blurred, and that makes it a very exciting time to be a woman, writing. I'm not someone who thinks that feminism has nothing left to say except to ask for equal pay and better childcare. I always thought feminism was about telling the world that women's experiences were just as valid and extraordinary as men's, and in some ways it's harder to do that when men and women are considered to be on some kind of emotional and psychological level playing-field together. Power play between the sexes, and within the same sex, is more complicated than ever but that makes life more exciting too, and more exciting to write about.

Glasgow isn't as hard and fast and competitive as London, Paris or New York, and it's still less culturally mixed than a great city should be. But it's a place that's changing all the time, and I think that's a good environment for any writer, man or woman. I never grew up thinking there were things I couldn't write about because I was a woman, or that my voice wasn't as valid as a man's, and I like to think some of that is down to where I come from.

Aschenputtel 07

Once upon a time, a man and a woman were married. They had two daughters, but the marriage was never happy and, eventually, they decided to part. The daughters lived with their mother, and their father went to live, on the same street in the same village, by himself. Many years later, he met another woman, and decided to marry again.

And this is where she comes in.

◈ ◈ ◈

The spider's speed sickened her. The wasp was floundering, caught in the stickiness of the web, struggling to free itself as that beady black body with its symmetrical white dots, a thing of beauty in many ways, scuttled across and spun it, round and round and round, until it was mummified by the membrane of the web. She watched, horrified, as the embalmed wasp, still alive, throbbed inside its tiny gossamer tomb, until, finally, it was still. Then the spider hauled it to the top of the web where it joined the window-pane, and sat, toying with its booty.

Ross would say that even in the city spiders kill wasps; it's not just in the country. But the three years since she left her high-ceilinged city flat for this country cottage with its low beams and squat doorways have not been long enough to lessen her repulsion at the extent, and the manner, of the countryside's sadism. The grouse and deer that are shot or lie senseless by the side of the road; the birds that screech and pick at the brown and red mingling of fox; the hedgehogs, rabbits and squirrels that are butchered or run over, their bones crushed and pulverised until they are no longer even solid matter, but some gluey, liquidised substance; no, she will never get used to any of it. Ross teases her about tasty meals made from road-kill, but she is vegetarian so anything he might want to put in the pot she wouldn't trust anyway.

She glimpses out of the window the woods at the back of the cottage. They are particularly dense – only once did she go mushroom-hunting there, when a neighbour told her there were plenty of chanterelles and ceps to be found, even some orange and some white birches. The woods are ochre, xanthic now; the rotting smells and colours of autumn may only be ever sweet and bright and beckoning, but she doesn't trust them either. She knows to find her way home by keeping to the shallow river which leads out of the woods and into the village, but she still got lost that one time, tracing and retracing her steps until it was almost nightfall and she really thought she was going to have to spend the night alone in the woods. Then she saw Ross's torchlight, knew she was safe.

She gets up slowly from the window-seat. She has been tired ever since the last round of IVF failed, and now that she is forty and Ross is fifty, she has given up any chance of their having children. It is lucky that she is so fond of Ross's daughters from his first marriage; Catriona and Mhairi were twelve and thirteen when she first met them, three years ago: pale-skinned, with the same delicate features and big, angelic blue eyes. Catriona has since grown the taller of the two; Mhairi has lost some of her babyish prettiness. But both are still light, graceful, beautiful, like fairy sisters wished upon her by a benevolent fairy godmother. She always wanted a little girl and even though they are not hers – their mother, Aileen, will never let her forget that – she can be their best friend; love them, if not like a mother, then at least like a favourite big sister.

The old range is on; Ross lit the fire before he went to work, as he does every morning. The kitchen table is still laden though with empty dishes, untouched since breakfast and lunch. She is struggling to rouse herself to do any housework at all. Then, suddenly, she hears familiar high-pitched voices, some girlish laughter, and footsteps crunching up the gravel outside.

Aileen attacked both her daughters with a pair of scissors, was the story. Neither Catriona nor Mhairi seem upset or shocked by what has happened; they are giggling now at their mother's crazy ways which they say have been getting crazier for weeks now. After running into the garden to get away from her, they called Ross on their mobile to come and rescue them. Why didn't you just come straight here? she asks them. They were too scared their mother would attack her too, they say, laughing. She is more distressed than they are; they can't go back home, she tells Ross. Aileen won't have them back, he says. And then something inside her lifts; she pictures her own bedroom at her parents' house, long since sold after they both died in a car crash, just over fifteen years ago. The doll's house; the Old English Sheepdog soft toy; the Pierrot duvet; the soft white furniture. Everything she wanted, she was given. Except for a little sister. She was her parents' only child; how she prayed every night for the little sister who never came.

◆ ◆ ◆

At first it was fun. Hearing the girlish voices calling to each other across the tiny landing from their rooms; listening out for their light, quick tread on the wooden stairs; treating them to the occasional glass of wine at dinner; letting them bring their boyfriends back so she and Ross could meet them. The girls have painted their rooms too, one in lavender, one in pale blue. There is no mention of them ever going back to their mother's.

But now, two months later, the week before Christmas, she has found herself for the fourth day in a row on her knees at the hearth like this, cleaning out the grate. Ross hasn't time to do it any more now that he has to drive the girls to their private school every morning, which is at the other end of town from his surgery. They have been keeping him busy, his girls, accompanying him to the village pub of an evening, or even when he's bird-watching in the woods – both things she had liked to let him do alone in the past. She shovels up the pink and grey ash, tips it into a box that she will later empty onto the special compost heap at the far end of the garden. She and Ross have hardly spent a moment alone since the girls arrived. She draws down strips of old newspaper, rolls them up to place inside the grate. When she came home from work last week, both girls were curled up on either side of him on the sofa. All three of them had a glass of red wine in their hands – the girls' was watered down, Ross assured her. None of them moved when she entered the room; no-one offered to pour her a glass of wine. Catriona and Mhairi simply smiled at her, curled up closer to their father. She didn't like the tiny resentments she felt inside her then. It wasn't fair to ask them to move; they had never had their father to themselves before, she told herself. She should be happy to make do with fetching her own wine, sitting in the easy-chair to the side.

She lifts out sooty chunks of coal, balances them carefully on the rolls of newspaper, before lighting a match and setting it under the pile of coal and paper. It's just little things, she tells herself, as she sweeps up the last of the ash. They have young taste-buds, that's why they hate vegetables and find her cooking dull, why they're always asking for a Macdonald's or some pizza. And yes, they did finish her one indulgence, a very expensive pot of face cream that Ross buys every year for her birthday, but that was an accident. And her organic clothing range is, she has to admit, a little frumpy, even for a woman her age. Catriona and Mhairi both like designer labels, and they insist she washes their expensive clothes by hand, with a special detergent, the way their mother used to. She has never been so busy before, hand-washing and ironing all their clothes; cleaning out their rooms; dusting all the furniture they've since had moved from their bedrooms at their mother's into their newly-painted ones at the cottage; trying to cook tasty new recipes for them. The drudgery is endless. Worse, Ross doesn't seem to have noticed.

She carries the container of old, cold ash outside. Ross is still paying full maintenance to Aileen, who does not work full-time as she does, even though the girls are living here now. She tries not to think about the money. She always wanted a family of her own. Now she is finding out what it is like, that's all. These are teething troubles, nothing more.

◆ ◆ ◆

Something had pecked out the dead cat's eyes. She couldn't tell what had killed it – a fox or a big dog, perhaps. But it lay on its side at the garden gate, its insides gashed and ripped open. Its upper lip was missing too. She knew she should bury it but just looking at it made her queasy. Nevertheless, she forced herself to go to the shed at the back of the garden and fetch a spade.

Ross and the girls are in town, at a gig the girls wanted to see. She was supposed to be going too, but then Catriona lost her ticket and as she hadn't wanted the girl to miss out, she had given Catriona hers. Otherwise Ross would be doing this now. She could still wait for him to come home and bury the cat, but it seems childish not to tackle it herself. It is light till almost seven now, it's not as if she'd be digging in the dark.

The cat's body is soft to the touch of the spade, and the softness seems to reverberate all the way to her hands. It is tricky to keep the cat on the shovel – its legs flop and as she fixes the spade under its shoulder, its head lolls back, tendons stretching, almost snapping. But she has to go on, and eventually the dead cat is lying on the shovel, its legs spilling out over the edges. Surprisingly heavy, horribly malleable, it drops like some ruined rag doll on to the earth behind the shed. She turns her back on it, begins to dig.

At last it is done. She puts the spade back in the shed and returns to the cottage. She runs a bath, sits down at the dressing-table in the bedroom, rubs her cheek. Its roughness is her second surprise that evening, and she stares at her reflection in the dressing-table mirror. Yes, she badly needs some moisturiser; her skin is rough and red, flaking at the hairline. She glances down at her hands – they are rough and red too. She runs them involuntarily through her hair, which is lank and greasy. When was the last time she had it cut? How long has she looked like this? All winter? No wonder she and Ross hardly have sex any more, although the girls' habit of barging in to their bedroom regardless of the hour has inhibited both of them. What has happened to her? It is no use asking Ross; he doesn't seem to notice what she wears or how she looks any more. Once upon a time, he did. Ross likes her best in forties-style dresses and skirts; she used to tease him for his old-fashioned taste. But with two teenage girls in the house, blossoming in a way she never did at that age, comparison is too great a risk. She is smothering her own sex appeal: that is what her face is telling her. And suddenly she starts to panic.

◆ ◆ ◆

Two weeks later, and for the first time since the girls arrived, she and Ross have the cottage to themselves. The girls are having a sleep-over at one of their friend's. Ross has come in, tired from work but astonished and pleased to see that she has cooked his favourite dish for him – rabbit stew – and is wearing a low-cut, red-and-black tea dress. She has put on weight over the winter – the girls are always teasing her about being fat – and few of her clothes fit any more, so she'd rushed into town and bought the kind of outfit she hardly ever wears, some moisturiser, a lipstick and a powder compact. Ross kisses her hand over dinner, strokes her powdered cheek. The candles melt down, the second bottle of wine is abandoned. With no-one to disturb them, she and Ross are naked, needy. Bodies, learning to touch again. Spooning the way they did, those first months after they met.

◆ ◆ ◆

The twelve weeks pass anxiously, but when she has her first scan everything, they say, is fine. Now, the girls can be told. It will mean, Ross says, driving haphazardly all the way back from the hospital, that the girls will either have to share a room, or even go back to their mother's, now that they are getting on so much better with her.

She doesn't say how much she wishes they would just leave. She says nothing at all.

Catriona and Mhairi are furious and disgusted with them both. How could they be having sex, at their age? Catriona refuses to move in with her sister, or return to her mother's. It is, she yells at them, not her fucking problem, slamming the door behind her. Mhairi follows, muttering threats, promising they will both regret it, that they have spawned a devil. She and Ross stare at each other; then Ross shakes his head. It's a huge shock for them, he says. They'll get over it.

Sixteen weeks later, when she stops in the village store for some milk and bread after one of her last days of work before maternity leave, she overhears two of her neighbours talking in the other aisle. They are discussing Catriona and Mhairi. The poor girls, one is saying, are having all sorts of problems with their stepmother. Their father's very unhappy, apparently. He's been trying to rid himself of her for ages. But now she's pregnant, she's got him trapped. Her companion murmurs, I never took to her. These city types. What she's put those girls through! Locking them in their rooms, I heard. Making them do all the housework while she sits around, stuffing her face. I thought she'd put on weight, even before the baby.

They move out of the shop; the door chimes as it closes behind them. She stands frozen, then drops her wire basket on the floor; hurries out after them. The single street is empty; did she imagine those women? Did she conjure that conversation out of nothing? She struggles along the road to the cottage; any walking is difficult now.

The girls are back from school already; they are sitting on chairs in the back garden. They each hold a white wine spritzer in a very large glass in one hand, a cigarette in the other. They are not allowed to drink when she and Ross are not present. And they are certainly not allowed to smoke. Mhairi deliberately blows smoke in her direction. She imagines her baby choking. And what have you two been saying to people behind my back? she accuses Catriona. Catriona stands up, and with a flick of her wrist, jerks the spritzer at her stepmother's swollen belly. Mhairi immediately runs after her sister, towards the cottage. She is left alone in the garden, white wine and soda spreading down her shirt.

The music coming from Catriona's room is unbearable, the insult added to the injury. She struggles up the wooden stairs, panting as she opens the door of Catriona's room. Catriona, huge blue eyes glittering in her summer-bronzed face. You're supposed to knock, you're not my fucking mother! She staggers to the stereo, bends down with difficulty, switches off the music. The silence, she will always remember in the months and years to come, is the warning. Suddenly Mhairi bares pretty, tiny white teeth, spits, put that back on, you bitch! Catriona's face, too, is distorted, full of loathing. Both sisters, once so beautiful, look ugly to her now. Get – out – of my – fucking – room, Catriona hisses, advancing towards her.

And something to do with babies and death and blood makes her snap suddenly; she picks up the nearest thing to hand, a small lamp that is unplugged, and hurls it across the room at her stepdaughter. You fucking mad cow, Catriona screams and leaps across the room, charges at her stepmother, grabs her by the shoulders, pushes her back through the open doorway. She is heavy though, at this last stage of her pregnancy, and she struggles, uses all her weight to push the teenager back. Catriona yells for help, Mhairi rushes over, together they are forcing her back, the staircase is behind her now, they are trying to push her down the stairs, they are pushing her harder and harder until her foot slips, she reaches out for the bannister but she misses it, she is in the air for just a second, she lets out a scream as she feels herself fall.

Behind her comes a strong arm, a firm body, a calm voice saying, I've got you, don't worry, I've got you.

◈ ◈ ◈

It was the shouting that made Aileen hurry into the cottage. She was passing when she heard her daughters screaming. She ran in, as fast as her bulky frame would allow, and saw her former husband's heavily pregnant wife at the top of the stairs, being attacked by her own daughters. Just as she had that day when they came at her with the scissors, she rushed at them now, blocking their stepmother's fall with her own body, holding the woman fast as she went down, cushioning her.

The girls moved back to their mother's house that evening, much to Ross's surprise, although he always knew, he told her, that in their own time they would see sense eventually. He has something for her, he says, as she lies quietly on the sofa, her hand resting on her abdomen. Both girls were christened in it, he tells her, as he hands over a white christening shawl, made entirely of lace, as intricately designed as a spider's web. And just for a moment, as she stares at his gift to her, she fancies she sees some small winged creature entangled inside it, its heart still beating. She blinks. But, no. It is just a trick of the light.

Patricia Ace

I was born in Cleethorpes to a Welsh father and West Indian mother but I spent periods of my childhood in Abu Dhabi, UAE and Calgary, Canada as well as in Surrey and Berkshire. My parents moved to Scotland in the mid-'80s and I spent holidays from school and London University with them in Aberdeen and Glasgow, where they are still based. I completed my first degree at Glasgow University and am currently back there again studying for an MLitt in Creative Writing. I settled in Perthshire in 1993. My partner is of solid Scottish stock and both my girls are born and bred in Scotland and very proud of it, too.

I have always been impressed by the energy and diversity of the Scottish literary scene and proud to be a part of it. In general, the writers, editors and publishers I have met have been welcoming and generous and Scotland a place where writers of all nationalities can flourish. Maybe this is to do with Scotland's history as a travelling and pioneering nation. I love the fact that Scotland produces both literature of gritty, urban realism and spiritual, rural lyricism, often inspired by the spectacular landscape. I think it's pretty special, as a nation, to have three languages at your disposal. I'm also always impressed by the willingness of Scottish writers to engage with ideas and politics so readily. Scottish writers have opinions and they aren't afraid to use them!

I've been introduced as a 'real feminist', although I've never seen myself in those terms. I make no apology for writing about women's experience of domesticity. It is always a part of any woman writer's life, especially those of us who bring up children. I got pretty fed up of being asked 'but what do you *do*?' when I eschewed a career in order to stay at home and bring up my daughters. I do feel that the careers of women writers can have a different trajectory to those of men. For instance, many women writers I have talked to said they only wrote poems (the least visible and least lucrative literary art form) when their children were small. I think women who write can come to the fore once their maternal responsibilities are less hands-on, although once you become a mother, you will never be completely free of these.

Patricia Ace

Talisman

You've cut out my tongue,
my Argonaut.

I'm silenced by your absence,
set adrift in the doldrums
that stretch between the text
you permit, like holes in fabric,
worried at, un-mended.

So you take leave
on another journey,
the far-flung four corners
calling to your wander-lust,
your need to be a hero,
your honour.

My tongue pinned to your prow,
pink-grey, tentacular, stitching
its stories in papyrus sails,
spitting its tales to the rigging.

I stand on the strand and watch
from the mainland the hull of your bark
slice the waves,
scissors through canvas.

Blood fills my mouth like ink.
I turn away to look for our sons.

Scottish Woman

(After 'Dying For It' by David Mach, 1989)

As if dropped from a height,
displayed in a thousand
whisky bottles, Scottish woman.

Saltire girl, bubble-wrapped
in glass. The empty vessels
stand to attention like soldiers,

supporting her creamy white
crime-scene form. Supine
in emulsion, she lies splayed.

Figurehead of a nation.
Displacing *aqua vitae*, she
keeps her head above water.

Laura Marney

Laura Marney is a nice person who tries to do a good deed every day. Occasionally bad deeds do slip in but there you go, nobody's perfect. Many of her short stories have been published in magazines and anthologies or broadcast on radio. She is the author of three novels: *No Wonder I Take a Drink, Nobody Loves a Ginger Baby* and *Only Strange People Go to Church*. Her next novel *My Best Friend Has Issues* will be published in July 2008. As well as writing for television, Radio 4 and occasional journalism, she is Deputy Convenor of the Creative Writing postgraduate MLitt course at Glasgow University.

Laura is a single parent whose own two children have recently flown the nest. She often dreams of them as small children and wishes they were so again but, on the other hand, she saves a fortune on spaghetti hoops.

Given that she had no choice in the matter, it was a happy accident that Laura Marney was born a woman. She feels doubly blessed to be a woman living in Scotland. She intends that this summer, or sometime soon anyway, she will travel around Scotland visiting the beautiful places she has not yet seen. She has spent a fortune on camping kit: tent, airbed, sleeping bag, gas stove, wind up radio and other essential camping gubbins that have not yet made it out of the packaging.

Laura Marney

This Side of Heaven

Iris

It's a lovely cornflower blue, so it is, and it'll go smashing with the wallpaper. I was going to buy it when I finished my shift but Margaret said no.

'Hang off a couple of weeks, Iris,' she said, 'just till you get your staff discount card. That way you get twenty percent off.'

I was worried in case they'd sell them all. Lamps like that go quick in Tesco.

'Here, I'll put it aside for you. Perks of the job,' Margaret whispered.

She's awful nice. Everybody's been nice.

When Jennifer comes home at the week end she's going to love what we've done with her room – *if* she comes home at the week end. The last time we had to drag her kicking and screaming out the place. I was mortified, so I was.

'Don't want to,' she said, stamping her feet like a spoiled princess. I could have wrung her neck, so I could.

She was crying when I put her coat on her. She'd been watching *X Factor* with her housemates and their carers before me and her dad had ruined her night. They were all sitting in the living room with popcorn and Coca Cola.

Jennifer keeps telling me that her and her housemates are the girls from *Friends*.

'So which one are you then?' I asked her, but she couldn't remember. She was desperate to tell me so we had to look it up online. She's getting really good at going online, better than me now, her flatmates and the carers in the house showed her. So we looked it up and apparently she's Monica.

'That's me there, Mum,' she said, 'She's got the same hair as me and she likes cleaning too.'

'Well you've got lovely dark hair and you're a maniac for cleaning so I suppose that's right enough,' I told her.

She gave me a big hug.

When she first went in to the house me and George had reservations, me more than him. Since Jennifer came out of school we've been talking about her having her own home.

'We'll have to face the facts, hen, we're not going to be around forever,' George always said. 'It's better to get her settled sooner rather than later.'

Even getting her on the list was a nightmare. George and me fought ten years to get Jennifer a place in a house. If we hadn't had the Greenies, I think we'd have given up a long time ago.

That's what we call ourselves: the Greenies. It's a helluva lot quicker than saying the Green Street Learning Disability Carers Group. The other Greenies have been great to us, so they have, we all help each other. My Jennifer, being that bit older than the other kids, has been the first to leave home so I suppose we're the guinea pigs. It's always been like that, I'm always the first to hear about a benefit or equipment that we might be entitled to, the Ringleader the rest of them call me. We pass the word around and if there's something we're not happy with we all complain together to the social work department: hold meetings, send petitions, that sort of thing. The whole crowd of us gets a lot more attention than if it was only one family.

You need to be organised, I learned that right from the minute Jennifer was born. You need to get all the support you can and the only people who really know where you're coming from is other parents of disabled children.

It wasn't until I started working in Tesco, when I saw all the nice House and Home electrical goods they have, that I realised. We've been so caught up in looking after Jennifer we've let modern life pass us by.

'We're a right pair of old fuddy-duddies, so we are,' I told George. 'I'm as bad as you. We've been living in a time warp.'

He nodded and smiled; he knew it was true. I haven't changed my hairstyle for more than twenty years. After Jennifer was born I got it cut short: low maintenance. I didn't have time for blow drying or anything fancy. The same with my clothes: jeans and a top every day, that's me.

When I saw the lovely bedroom they'd given Jennifer I nearly cried. It was all done out in baby pink with curtains and lamps to match. It's just a perfect girl's room and she loves it.

'We have to learn from our daughter,' I told George. 'If Jennifer can change and move forward then so can we.'

I have to admit he surprised me.

'Well it's not as if we can't afford it,' he said. 'With you working we've a wee bit more money coming in. You're right, we're not pensioners. We should get with the groove.'

I didn't argue. The minute I got my staff discount card I went to town with it. I bought the lovely blue lamp and a new duvet cover.

'We'll see if this meets with Her Majesty's approval,' I said.

George laughed.

'By the way, Margaret was telling me there's a staff night out at the end of the month. She asked if I was coming.'

'Knock yourself out,' said my loving husband.

'Charming,' I said. 'Anyway, I've nothing to wear.'

'Well buy yourself something, and while you're at it get your hair done. And when you come back from your night out, couple of drinks, know what I mean?'

'Know what?' I said.

'Well: new clothes, new hairdo, no Jennifer in the house. You know what you're like with a few drinks in you. You'll probably be waking me up, wanting to get fruity.'

I laughed.

'Away you go out with your new pals,' he said, digging me in the ribs.

'Och, I don't know, it'll feel weird going out enjoying myself.'

'Well, Iris,' George said, 'that's what normal people do all the time.'

Rose

It was as if she'd died.

I remember what it was like when my man died and it was worse than that; worse than if Heather had died. It still is. D'you think I don't want my daughter at home with me? I'd gi'e anythin' to be able to look after her mysel'. I'm the only one who knows how to. Some of the care staff do a good job, but they're no' her mam. They're in there on a minimum wage for a couple of hours a week. You cannae compare that against thirty years lovin' attention from her own mam.

Heather's no' an easy girl to get to know. They telt me to write it doon. I've written oot sheets and sheets to try and explain what she's like: what makes her angry and what makes her happy or sad, but they cannae understand her the way I can. They don't know all her funny wee moods, what she's trying to tell you when she makes those wee signals with her hands and her eyes.

I wasnae prepared. I was on that waiting list fifteen years and next thing I know they're offering me a place for Heather. It comes down to health and safety, Dr Gray said; we've got a big daughter with a wee mum and that's a problem. Heather's twice your weight. Osteoarthritis is progressive, it won't get any easier and your situation is not only untenable, it's becoming dangerous. We'll need to arrange things soon; they won't hold the place open for long, or the funding. Somebody else will snap it up.

I'd no choice.

Heather was devastated. The first time I saw her after she'd gone in I burst oot greetin'. So did she. She looked terrible. She hadnae been sleepin', they telt me. She'd started bitin' again. She was bitin' herself in her sleep and there was naebody there to stop her. She had a big scab on her right arm. She'd put her teeth through the skin and it got infected. She didnae like the food they were giving her either. I kept telling them she'll no' eat pasta but she'd lost two stone before they sorted it oot. They kept telling me it was okay. They've got a hoose manager up there, Barbara, and she called in a dietician and a community disability nurse when there was all the bother with Heather not eatin'. They've had meetin' after meetin' but they don't tell me what's going on. I'm the last to know anything.

They told me she'd be in with two other females. I thought Heather would like that. I thought she'd make friends with the other two, it would be company for her, but it's no' like that. Heather doesnae like anybody in the house, she sleeps all day, she's less sociable now than ever she was.

So am I, come to that. I don't go near the carer's club any more. What for? I'm no' a carer, no' noo. The benefits folk were quick enough to tell me that. They gave me six weeks to get on my feet and then they took away all the benefits. Mary told me I'm still welcome at the club but I feel I shouldnae be there. The rest of them have still got their own ones to worry about, they don't need me hangin' aboot like a bad smell. Parents of kids with learning disabilities havenae got their troubles to seek, that's for sure, but at least they've got a purpose in life. What purpose have I got?

When Heather went into the home I didnae know what to do with myself. It felt like when my man died but at least when my man died that was it: over, finito, good night Vienna. The grievin' was hard, part of the process, you cannae expect anything else, but after a year or two I accepted it, I got over it. I willnae get over this. Before he went he asked me if I believed in the afterlife. He knew fine well I wasnae religious, I never have been, but I telt him I hoped that there would be something.

After he died Mary and me started goin' to meetin's at the spiritualist church. Everybody there had lost a dear one. Everybody was sad but we were all sad together. It was nice. Mary was gettin' messages every other week from her mother and her brother tellin' her that they were fine and no' to worry. A couple of months after Heather had gone into the hoose, after she'd lost all that weight and went right downhill, the medium had a message for me. It was from my man, to tell me he was fine and no' to worry.

I never went back after that.

I try no' to be all doom and gloom but I get cold shivers when I think aboot the future. I can't help thinkin' that maybe Heather bein' in the home is gonnae shorten her life. Everythin' I warned them aboot has come true. I knew her seizures would get worse and I was right.

It's no' even as if I can talk to Heather aboot why she has to be in there. She just thinks I don't want her. That's the worse thing. She doesnae understand. At least with my man I could help him try to understand things. When I said I thought we were goin' to a better place I said it to comfort him. This life is shite enough, my man said, surely the next must be better. We had a laugh aboot that.

If only Heather could understand that and hold on to that hope.

If only I could believe it mysel'.

Daisy

The first thing I did when Richard died was sell the house. As a young couple we'd scrimped to pay the mortgage but Richard worked hard building up the business and we eventually paid it off. The estate agent said the area was highly desirable and the house would fetch a good price, but I'd get more if it was re-decorated.

The house had got a bit dowdy over the years. Don't get me wrong, not neglected, it was a house full of love, it was our home and we were very happy, but when you have a disabled child things like this season's wallpaper fashions become rather low priority.

I got a quote from a painter and decorator but I didn't have that kind of money. Believe me, you can work wonders with a couple of litres of B&Q paint and a roller. Over a couple of weeks while Jacqueline was at day care I did all eight rooms myself. A blank canvas, the estate agent said, so I chose magnolia. By the time I was finished I had magnolia hands, magnolia clothes, magnolia hair. I was so well camouflaged that if I stood against the wall Jacqueline had a job finding me. I painted every surface in the house, everywhere but the kitchen door frame. I couldn't paint over that.

On Jacqueline's birthday Richard and I always had our own family ritual. We'd put a ruler on her head and draw a line across the kitchen door frame. Then we'd measure it and record her height and age along the line. One year she grew more than two inches. Jacqueline used to drag visitors into the kitchen to show them. She was always very proud of how grown up she was becoming.

The estate agent was right. I got a great price for the house. I used some of the money to buy a smaller place, a tiny flat with two bedrooms. Jacqueline receives benefits but it's simply not sufficient to pay for the care she needs. Selling the house released capital which helped pay for a day service package with 'tuck in'. I count my blessings. Many other parents of disabled children don't have these resources and I thank Jesus every day.

It's true that I'm getting older but I have no fear of death, quite the reverse. I do worry about leaving Jacqueline, but my faith sustains me, the Lord will provide. I live very carefully and I've put the rest of the money in trust for when I go to God.

Sometimes while Jacqueline is out with a carer I take the bus and go back and look at our old house. I only look, that's all I do. There's a bench opposite the house facing the park and I sit there. I don't want to pry. I wonder if the new people have painted the kitchen door frame; I suppose they must have.

On her twentieth birthday Richard and I measured Jacqueline but she was the same height. We did the same the next year but she'd stopped growing. She was disappointed. I don't mark the door frame in this flat. Luckily she seems to have forgotten about it. Suffer the little children to come unto me, said Jesus. Jacqueline is thirty-seven next Friday. She'll always be a little child.

Since Richard died Jacqueline has been such a comfort to me. When I look into her lovely eyes I see Richard there and know I am blessed. She's a happy-go-lucky girl. Her life is busy with activities. She loves going swimming and horse-riding. Generally she gets on well with her carers. She loves to play her music. The walls are paper-thin here; it must drive our neighbours mad. We go out to the park to feed the ducks, and to art galleries, although she sometimes gets bored. She's a big fan of athletics and gymnastics on television, and of recent years we've travelled to the big sports meetings. We've met one or two of our heroes and they always make a big fuss of Jacqueline. On Sundays she comes to church with me. She's such a fidget I don't get a chance to pray in peace, so the minister has arranged for other parishioners to sit with her during the service. I'm very lucky.

It's a constant struggle trying to juggle Jacqueline's benefits and arrange her care. I like to think I've organised a pool of good carers and put solid procedures in place to protect my daughter, but I don't know. I'm not trained in this kind of thing. I'm just a housewife, but I've had to become a finance expert, a legal expert, a negotiator, a fund raiser, an administrator and a full-time project manager. It doesn't leave a lot for time for just being Mummy. Sometimes I think I'm too old and I haven't got the energy for it any more. At these dark times the weight of responsibility overwhelms me and I wish Jacqueline could go into care. It's too much responsibility for one person. But I know God has given me this work for a reason. I must accept the things I cannot change. I must get on with it. I look forward to a time when we'll all be with Jesus: me, Richard and Jacqueline together.

Jacqueline has a comfortable home. For the present she has Mummy. God sends us the carers we need and gives me the strength to cope. It's not perfect but it's the nearest thing we're going to get this side of heaven.

Violet

Listen, I'm not bloody kidding. The social work department will have to do something for Andrew. It's your legal and moral obligation. You've been telling me for years that you haven't got the places. You keep telling me about flexible choices. I'm fed up hearing it. Choices and benefits and grants. These things are no use to me. How do I know how to take on carers, pay them their wages, sort out their holiday pay? I don't want money, I need a place for my son. You're always talking about choices, trying to make it sound like it's a good thing but as far as I can see you're just trying to bloody dump it on me. The government thinks it's cheaper to give me money and wash their hands of people like Andrew. And I'm here to tell you, he's not going away. Aye, I know the cost implications of re-housing him, you've told me. Do you know the cost implications of *not* re-housing him? D'you know how much I'm saving this government? I'll tell you, me and people like me are saving you £57 billion. Now, see all that money we're saving you? Well it's payback time. Not for me, for Andrew. He needs a place where he can live in comfort and safety, that's all we want, and this time, by Christ, we're going to bloody get it. Look, I know every time you see me you just see this nut-case shouting, swearing woman, but I wasn't always this angry.

I already had three kids when I had Andrew, so I should have spotted something was wrong right away, but I just thought he was lazy. We had him up at the hospital four or five times and I still had no idea what was going on. They don't tell you nothing.

They gave me a letter to take from one department to another and on the way I nipped into the toilet and opened it. I opened it dead carefully so they wouldn't know. Severe mental handicap, it said. I took it to the consultant right away. I was that upset I forgot to seal it up again.

They wanted to put him in hospital, for good. You're a young woman, they said, put it behind you, go home and look after your other children. It sounds like something out of Dickens, doesn't it? But my hand to God, that's what they said to me: go home and forget about him. I looked at him lying sleeping in the pram, he was just a wee baby, a beautiful curly-haired wee thing.

I said to my husband we'd manage; we've already got three, what's another one to look after? It's only another tottie in the pot. He didn't see it that way. He was gone within the year. Andrew never missed him, but I felt bad for the other three.

I'm on my own with him twenty-four hours a day. His brother and two sisters were a good help but they've got their own families now. They've already lost out so much when they were young, no dad around and all my time taken up with looking after Andrew, I've always felt guilty about that. I don't want to burden them. I wasn't much of a mother to them and so far I've not been much of a granny.

I get lonely in the house on my own but the internet's been a great thing for me. I go online when he's sleeping and talk to other folk in the chat room. That's how I know how much money we're saving you. That's how I know what Andrew's entitled to. I might be stuck in the house but I'm well-informed, we all are. Everybody feels the same. We're all struggling to pay bills, a lot of us don't keep well, we're fed up of being fobbed off with excuses, we're all angry.

Look, I might not have a posh accent or live in a fancy house but I'm not daft. I know you're strapped for money and houses to put kids in. I know it would be better for you if I just went home and didn't make a fuss. But it wouldn't be any good for Andrew. And that's why I'm leaving him here. I'm walking out of this office. His medicine is in this bag on the back of his chair. I've told the newspaper. They took a photo of me and Andrew outside. I'm not making a protest, I'm calling a strike. I'm not the only one. I've got together with thousands of other people online; we're all doing it. This way you'll have to do something. We've prepared a statement and I want you to listen to it and then I'm walking out of here, without Andrew. Here goes.

As of 11 am this morning I, and thousands of other parents and carers of adults with learning disabilities throughout Britain, formally hand over responsibility for the health-care and wellbeing of our sons and daughters to the Social Work Department. Our reasons are that we are poor, we don't have any political clout, and the government leaves us to struggle alone with what is sometimes an impossible task. The only bargaining chip we have is the hundreds of hours of unpaid care we each do. That's why we are withdrawing our labour until you start to listen. We do not have formalised demands, our needs are different and so we ask that each case be looked at individually. We do not do this lightly. We understand the pain and confusion this will cause. We know what people will think of us. We love our kids and it's because we love our kids that we can no longer be emotionally blackmailed into accepting the unacceptable. We have been pushed to our last resort. It's over to you. Our kids are the most precious thing in the world to us, please take good care of them, we can't do it on our own any more.

Yvonne Gray

When I was growing up, Scottishness was to do with having, in one way or another, the wrong accent. I was born in Ayrshire and grew up in Renfrewshire, Lanarkshire and Midlothian, realising with each move that the way I spoke was different – that there were other ways of pronouncing things, other names for the games we played.

I studied English at Edinburgh University. When a tutor suggested taking Scottish Literature one year I was doubtful – apart from Burns and Scott, what was there to study? Later these (green) shutters opened out onto a much wider cultural landscape – coloured vividly by writers from Orkney to the Western Isles, from the Borders to Caithness. I heard the varieties of Scots around me in a new way, varied and expressive instead of debased and (as I'd assumed at school) rightly derided. Scottish writers were, however, all *men*, a notion that lingered until the mid-eighties, when I saw the growing number of Scottish women being published.

In 1990 my husband got a job in Orkney where he had family connections; we moved and settled near Stromness with our three sons. I've lived in Scotland all my life and yet the question 'where do you come from?' is difficult to answer. I used to envy the sense of belonging to a *particular* place which many people have. Now, though, I think that *not* belonging is a valid position too, and has its own wellspring.

I try to balance family life with part time work as an English teacher. I love music and play the oboe when I can. Music practice and writing are both solitary activities though, and I enjoy the stimulus and shared experience of performing and collaborating with artists of different sorts.

Yvonne Gray

St Magnus Festival Poet
(with Exposed Painting, Charcoal Black/Red Oxide by Callum Innes)

for Jackie Kay

You stand at the end of the long pier gallery
framed by a painting sectioned squarely
into planes of white and black and light tan.
Did it happen by chance, or did you plan
to stand and read your poems just there,
your head on the interface, with your short black hair,
snow white teeth and liquid honey-gold skin?
The space you inhabit, you seem at home in.
A tall (black) man in the row in front turns
to his short (white) companion to murmur
She's wonderful – then smiles to me, an incomer
to the island with sons neither weans nor bairns
(though I'm moved to hear my Ayrshire grandmother
speak again when you say the words *gien it laldy*).

Yggdrasil

You came north in winter, car loaded, the sun
Going steeply down. The earth was tilting, darkness
Growing. The road swung as you mapped your route
Driving up a spindly line of longitude, a thread that left you
Reeling – cast off on a fringe of islands scattered at the
Atlantic edge. You never saw the juniper tree, low branches
Spreading across the wind-swept moor, as it threaded
Its bole into the peat, an axle through the earth.
Leaving, you headed south, steadier as the light returned.

Linda Cracknell

I first came to Scotland on a field trip from Exeter Art College in Midsummer 1979. We stayed at a hostel in Elphin. The idea was to paint but I mostly walked – I couldn't *not* walk. I remember how the landscape gnawed at me, took me to the top of Cnoc Breac at midnight, swimming in the dark at Clashnessie. It started something.

I came back with my partner most summers – walking trips to Skye or the Western Isles, always the far north-west at first. I kept notebooks. Sketches, scribblings of words started to appear.

In 1990 we moved to Scotland, both of us involved with work in the Central Belt. In 1995 I got a job with WWF and moved to Perthshire. My hand had been itching. I signed up for a creative writing course with Open College of the Arts. And that started something.

In 1998 I won the Macallan/Scotland on Sunday short story competition with *Life Drawing,* and in 2000 a collection of the same title was published. By this time, I couldn't *not* write. A three-year writing residency at Hugh MacDiarmid's last home, Brownsbank Cottage, gave me a bridge into a freelance life. I wrote drama and stories for BBC Radio, ran workshops with schools and writers' groups. In early 2008 *The Searching Glance,* a second short story collection was published.

Paths and memory-lines in the land continued to lure my feet and set my hand scribbling. As Rebecca Solnit says of the literature of walking: '... the necessary combination of silver tongue and iron thighs seems to be a rare one'. In 2007 I won a Creative Scotland Award to walk and write a series of journeys. Through imagination, memory, myth, history, I am exploring the human resonances layered in 'wild' land.

And that's how this piece came to be ...

www.lindacracknell.blogspot.com

Linda Cracknell

Cailliche

After crossing to Skye, I found myself tight-rope walking on the cusp of the Autumn Equinox. I wasn't at all sure that I would continue my journey.

For the previous thirteen days, the promise of Camasunary had gleamed at the end of the walk – my ultimate camping spot in a sweep of bay under the Cuillins on the south of the island, a place of close-cropped grass, a hollow between two ridges, a beach, a haven. I had imagined myself relaxing there in sunshine, watching birds and reading.

But to include Camasunary meant another two days' walking, and with the prospect of further raging weather, I was ready to call it a day. I could honourably consider my journey complete, after all it had been my main intention to reach Skye. I found shelter from the rising force eight in a Broadford B&B and from there considered next steps.

The next morning Philip Tordoff, my host, stood outside the door with me, continuing our conversation about the value of walking the old ways, about what it means to find enlightenment in land and books. Trained as a church minister, he had a soft way of laying words, and I felt my path strangely blessed by him as he offered advice on places on my route. I walked off into a dry morning, gusted past the Co-op, and my boots strode me back into a rhythm. Rather than turning for home, I faced south-west towards Elgol, and the road rose to meet me.

'In particular,' he had said, 'be sure to take a small detour, climb the hill next to where a red van is parked.'

This chance meeting was how I came to visit High Pastures, one of the several treasures in the casket of that particular day. And Philip Tordoff joined the ranks of my esteemed guides. Foremost amongst them were the drovers – intelligent, hardy businessmen who fashioned the route with understanding of human and animal movement, weather, watercourses and sources of hospitality. They found firm ground and food for the cattle. Their confidence in the best ways through the land later led to stones paved over their line, and later still, in some places such as here, tarmac. The drovers showed me the way and lent weight and history to my own journey. Their voices were faint now, but not their tracks, deeply etched in a memory-line of feet and hooves.

Strath Suardal cradles the Broadford River, and there the bold, lumpen mass of Beinn na Caillich watched me as I walked the windswept valley towards the red van. The hill altered little in shape as I passed south. Eroded and rounded out of red granite unlike the gabbro-corrugated Black Cuillin that I was heading for later that day, it framed itself within the doorway of Cill Chriosd, the ivy-tangled roofless church that sits on an ancient mound.

The cailliche[1] – the old woman or hag goddess – played a central role in a story I had written three years earlier[2]. Loosely set on one of my local hills, Schiehallion, she was losing her power as Beltane marked the arrival of Spring. She was a goddess of Winter with knuckly cold fingers and a blue face, spreading ice, shattering rocks and clutching at human hearts. In my version, she was attended by creaking herons. The honk of geese heralding her arrival at Samhain and departure at Beltane would be more traditional. In my story, and I suppose in my mind, she was to be feared, a mere hoarse whisper away from death.

The cailliche had been showing herself to me over the summer, cropping up in place names and folkloric stories, her face outlined on the southern headland at the entrance to Loch Broom and in the names of mountains such as this in Strath Suardal.

I am not an old woman, and yet if you are considered old once your fertile years are past, I'm heading towards that different way of being. This journey was challenging my body, calling for stamina, energy, strength, mobility – qualities of youth. Just before setting off I had received a letter from my surgery, telling me a test result showed I may have 'joint disease'. I knew the meaning of the two words individually, but together they meant little. As I held the letter, a picture lurched into my mind of an old man I had seen inching along a pavement, so bent over that he could not look ahead. His wife was leading him, being his eyes. I remembered that I had bounded past them. I put the letter under a pile of other papers to consider on my return.

Not much beyond the churchyard, near where the road turns west and northwest towards Torrin, I left my rucksack and followed the markers uphill from the red van. On the hill or 'high pastures', deep underneath the shielings of a more recent people, a system of caves has concealed ritual mysteries of female fertility. Poised between limestone and granite, where water dives and vanishes into the earth, archaeologists are discovering in layers of ash the story of a fire kept burning for eight hundred years. Where daylight hits the womb-shaped cave floor, objects associated with the Celtic goddess Brigid have been buried.

In this underworld, buried treasure tells of transitions. At the cave entrance – the interface of light and dark – there are quern-stones that made flour from grain, iron-smelting equipment that changed rock to metal. Bones glimmer, highlighting the point between life and death. Around 80 AD the site was ritually filled in, and the cave entrance topped with the skeleton of a young woman, the remains of a five-month-old foetus and a two-week-old child.

There were people kneeling in trenches, scraping carefully at layers of history, straining soil through water to look for clues. They seemed eager to speak about the uncovering of memory. The scent of discovery was palpable. A woman told me she had come all the way from South Africa to volunteer for six weeks on the dig. There were a few of us visiting the site, hanging on the words of the archaeologists. We stood out of the wind in a wooden hut, prickled by an incredible story and the questions it raised. 'Could it be …?' 'What if …?' We added our speculations to theirs and then grew quiet, thoughtful.

We were balancing at a season of equal dark and light, in a place where the world above meets the world below, and on a geological boundary. I think we all felt a profound moment under our feet.

Outside the shed, a white stone stood on the grass. Perhaps two and a half feet high, it had a wide base and a narrowing upright body, shaped into curves and edges like a seated figure. Moulded by water and then buried below, it seemed to have as much in common with a sculpture by Henry Moore or Barbara Hepworth as with Bronze Age remains.

The stone begged questions. But it also led me back to another place, to which Iain had been my guide ten days earlier.

The ridge linking Beinn Achaladair and Beinn a' Chreachain

drains through Glen Meran and Gleann Cailliche into the north-west finger of Loch Lyon. With Iain and Sue I had climbed west into Glen Cailliche. It was a small deviation from my route which would later take me through Glen Meran and onto Rannoch Moor.

Near the burn, amongst green pastures, we found the small house, 'Tigh nam Bodach'. Perhaps two feet high including its turf roof, it has stone walls and a paved floor. Because we were there during the six months of light, the stones of the front wall had been lifted clear to open the house, and seven odd stone figures stood in two lines in front of it.

Worried and licked into curious shapes by burn water, the figures appeared to represent a family. The woman dominated the group. She had a wide, squarish base that narrowed at the top into a thin neck, and a spherical head, coloured pink. The rest of her brood – smaller and less solid apart from one wide squat one – were also fashioned by the differential wear of water to give their upper edges rims or lines. They stood with the strength and dignity of figures on Easter Island.

We sat just downhill of them and stared. With low cloud obscuring the high ridge, the sides of the Cailliche valley met perfectly at the roof of the house. In a windswept but fertile-green place, the house is said by some to be a 'shieling shrine'[3]. The first thing that would be done as the party arrived each year to graze the cattle, make cheese, tell stories, was to open up the house and bring out the figures. But even now, the ritual opening and closing of the house is continued at the two ends of the year.

We pondered what force it was that would bring a modern-day keeper up on his quad bike to officiate. We wondered what it meant that something which spoke of fertility was positioned by the burn and glen that take the name of an *old* woman. Is it that the three phases of womanhood – girlhood, fertility and age are gathered in one place?

We lingered there a long time just below the cloud base, putting our hands on the rough, lichen-grained stones as if they would give us answers. An earthy reverence held us there. When we did walk away through the long grass to the track above the loch, we stopped often to look over our shoulders at the small powerful presence.

The image of the bold stone woman had stayed with me. She had given me my 'send-off' as I crossed my first real threshold into the unsettled west out of my 'home glen', when Iain and Sue turned for home. Now, here at High Pastures where orange tape marked the edges of the excavation and enthusiasts scrabbled at discovery with cold earth ingrained in their hands, she seemed to show herself again, just as I neared the end of my two-week-long journey. The pale rock sculpted by water sat rounded and solid.

Before I left I asked the archaeologist for his name. 'Martin Wildgoose,' he said. Of course, I thought, and heard again skein-cries of migration marking the change in the year. I cast a wry nod at Bein na Caillich. The hag-goddess was prowling nearby, waiting to be heralded in again by her geese.

I walked back down the grassy slope towards my rucksack, the road, the way ahead. My enthusiasm for journeying had been refreshed. A small figure in a red cagoule moved very slowly ahead of me. It took the road in the same direction as me, the hood up, arms splaying a bit awkwardly at its sides. It seemed to list like an overloaded boat lashed at by the wind. I caught up quickly and when the figure turned at my greeting, I saw it was the elderly woman who had been in the hut when I arrived at the dig, asking a great many questions. We exchanged a few words of marvel at what we had witnessed up there and then she told me to go on, otherwise she would hold me up, and it was raining.

I did go on, eager to make some headway on the ten miles of road I had to march before the up-and-over on the track to Camasunary. I was also eager to get to the café. I wondered how far the old lady was going.

The village of Torrin hugs a low slope on the eastern side of Loch Slapin. I descended through it, enjoying its bright green meadows and effervescent fertility. Sprays of orange monbretia startled against the white cottages. On the other side of the loch the fierce fortress of Bla Bheinn thrust up its craggy skyline, black and gothic.

I sat out several heavy showers in the Blue Shed Café, drank coffee, had soup and toasties. An old BMW motorbike was parked outside, its unconventionally towering luggage flapping string and black plastic. Inside, a tall man with a posh English voice, long wavy brown hair and a weather-beaten face was holding court with a couple on another table. He talked of his journey, about sub-prime mortgages, the world economy, his life story. I wrote in my journal, looked out as sheets of rain obscured and then shimmered on Bla Bheinn's striated and gully-scarred rocks. In the middle of the day a warm fug of travellers' conviviality steamed the windows of the café. Each new arrival had to be helped with the damp-stuck door.

After about forty-five minutes the woman in the red cagoule arrived and we were soon sharing a table, she encouraging me to eat cake. She wore a blue jumper which matched her eyes. She never stopped smiling. There was a sense of great intelligence about her at the same time as a vagueness, an other-worldliness. We talked about what we were both doing, her adventures that week on local buses around Youth Hostels on the island. She told me how, by living in a retirement apartment in Edinburgh, she had lost the stars in the night sky to a halo of orange security lighting. But in certain places, at night on Arthur's Seat, she could still find true dark, even in the City. She told me of her former love of walking, and we spoke of unconventional lifestyles.

I told her how a man at a similar table in a Glen Lyon café had said my lifestyle sounded like retirement and how friends tell me I appear to be on holiday all the time whilst I feel I never can be 'on holiday'. My life is filled with vocation that has no nine-to-five, that is both play and work, that can never be put aside even in sleep, and whose grip on me I love and occasionally resent.

'People just think that it can only be work if it makes you miserable,' she said. 'Ignore it.' She seemed to understand with almost no explanation what I was doing and why.

It was as if in the time we talked a tide that had gone out, came splashing and tumbling back onto the shore. If my journey had been in question the night before, my way lost, I was now back on course. Kindled by Philip Tordoff's blessing, and fed by 'High Pastures', my commitment was breathed into flame by meeting this woman. I felt restored from the wounded weakness of the previous night.

When she stood up to catch her bus back to Uig, she paused, and made sure I was listening.

'I have arthritis now, it's stopped me. But please, keep doing it,' she said. 'Keep walking. For just as long as you can.'

And I promised her that I would.

I was rummaging in my rucksack outside the café when I heard the blue Highland bus growling up the hill behind me. I turned around. There was only one passenger on it, seated near the front. At the same moment, each of us threw an arm high in the air in an affectionate salute. I followed the bus with my eyes until it was out of sight.

In this brief meeting some fundamental connection seemed to have sprung between us. Perhaps I had seen the woman I hope I will be in my seventies and she had seen someone she used to be. As she headed north-east past Cill Chriosd and up the valley to Broadford, I knew that a tall broad hill would watch the bus pass at its feet along the single track road. I began to understand that in her simplest form, the cailliche represents a different stage of life. I thought of this woman as my cailliche, and I no longer felt afraid.

This is an extract from a longer piece, 'The Dogs' Route', about a fifteen-day walk following drovers between Perthshire and Skye taken by the author in September 2007. It is part of a project enabled through a Creative Scotland Award supported by the National Lottery through the Scottish Arts Council.

[1] also spelt 'cailleach'

[2] *The Weight of the Earth and the Lightness of the Human Heart*, in *The Searching Glance*, Salt 2008

[3] http://www.rcahms.gov.uk/canmore/details_gis?inumlink=23898

Sharon Blackie

Like so many others among these pages, I am something of a mongrel. My father's family is Scottish as far back as anyone has ever been able to discover, their roots in Midlothian and Edinburgh. My mother's family is part-English, part-Irish. I admit only to the Celtic genes. I also, in some sense, feel dispossessed of that Scottishness. My father, brought up in a tenement slum in Granton, associated Edinburgh only with poverty and negative memories. The irony is that he ended his days in a run-down council estate in Middlesbrough ... but I, as a child, was consequently deprived of the only place I ever wanted to live. Growing up in my mother's home town, a dismal steel-town in the north-east of England, I loved to visit our relatives in Edinburgh. To me it was Oz: a far-off magical city, exotic and stunningly beautiful. It still feels that way to me now.

It took me a good while to work my way back to Scotland, driven always from country to country, house to house by a travelling bug that has been with me most of my life. But I'm drawn to edges of things; my feet point north and west. Scottish isn't a matter of accent; perhaps it's a matter of orientation. So maybe it was inevitable that, in 2003, I came to a six-acre croft on the shores of Loch Broom and gave up my wanderlust to settle in this place for what feels like it's going to be forever. I can *be* here; and whether I was born here or not, at some much deeper level, I can belong. In this small, remote crofting community, no-one has ever seemed to think it especially strange that a woman should turn up one day, at that time all by herself, and occupy a croft that had effectively been abandoned for forty years.

And now, with a husband and a dog and a cat and ten sheep and three geese and thirty-odd hens (not to mention the small matters of a publishing company to run and a writing career to progress) life is rarely dull. My first novel, *The Long Delirious Burning Blue* (Two Ravens Press, 2008), was a product of this place and of the space that I can find here.

www.sharonblackie.com

Here

There's a mystery to fish, you said, *to trout. What is it that makes one trout a brown trout and another a sea-trout? Every trout that is born has the potential to be either. Why is it, then, that one fish will stay in the lochs and the rivers and another will head off to sea? Off to sea and no-one knows what happens to them, no-one knows where they go.*

And here we stand in this fledgling morning, the dawn still to come as we stand on the dark shore in our waders. No sound now except the sound of our breathing; the softest whisper of a breeze to ruffle the feathers of the water, flickering in the slowly fading moonlight. Orion no more than a glimmer, hunter hanging over hunter. Here we stand, not shipwrecked yet, washed up on a tide of longing that we could never admit to, not us, for aren't we stronger than that? Glass vessels built for messages that we have not yet learned to decode.

We step into the waiting water, slowly slip forward, sand soft under our feet. Stealthily, furtively, not to startle the silvery fish who, drowsing gently in his bed of boulders, may yet arise from his slumber of sea-dreams to feast on a breakfast of death. An outraged wail breaks into the silence; a lapwing circles above our heads. We edge in closer, up to our waists now, as the loch rearranges itself around us. I sway a little in the dark, sway outside myself and into the dark flow of the water, following the flow and dark shadows swoop around us, harsh calls and a startling splash as the greylags land at the mouth of the loch. From air to water and back to air again, always changing, always moving on. The soft whip of the line as you cast it to see if the trout sleeps still, the old sea-rover now returned to all his childhood haunts. *And what of those that stay behind*, I think of asking, but we are sea-trout you and I, neither in this loch nor out of it, neither of it nor apart from it, and how can it be that a pool of water can harbour this much mystery?

You move on forward, head cocked, mouth open, as if you can taste your way to the fish, as the questing trout will taste the rivers to find his way back home. No selkies here in your world, just fish, and yet the water dissolves our skin and becomes us and the process of becoming never ends... The sun is stirring behind us now, it rises up and lifts the morning into being ... a sea wind begins to whip up slowly, an old familiar desire caressing the surface of the loch ... and a single small tug on your line as the fish plays you, for the fish knows what I want to say to you but do not, for fear of breaking this wild silence. Listen, I want to say to you – listen. This is what it all comes down to; this is what it is for. The wild geese crying overhead; the soft silver kiss of a fish as it slips on by in its dawning dream of the gravels. Two people, waist-high in a dark icy loch, and a world in which even a fish can choose who it wants to be.

Listen

Listen.

Can you hear Him?

Of course you can't hear Him; He only speaks to me. All that you'd hear is the trace of a whisper – the slightest of traces, a sigh in the leaves. A long slow *shhhh* and then there's a *whshhh* and that light breathy laughter fading on the breeze... I could translate it for you, but I won't.

His words are all for me.

I'd never have thought I would find Him here – on this dark island forsaken by all gods, this stunted place, chopped off and chopped up and barren, this flat moss-covered pebble in the middle of a giant sea and I can't swim.

Whshhh and shhhh and love and laughter and where have you gone to, Marnie Moon?

Marnie Moon, loony tune. Marnie because it's the name I was born with; Moon for my fear of it when I was small. Big white shining ball in the sky – light, too light, face smirking down, *I see you – I see you, Marnie Moon.* Up in the sky – scary sky. Sun and moon and stars and sky and all of them watching me, spying and seeing me.

No place to hide.

No place to hide on this island.

No place to hide and the sky pressing down on you pressing you flat, flat to the earth and the holes in the sky that they shine their lights through, shine them down and watch you, see you.

Weight of the sky, grey and leaden. There's nothing here to hold up the sky. It sags and it folds like a dirty grey blanket and you cannot hold it off you cannot hold it up it will fall on you one day, Marnie Moon. And the wind here kills you with tender blows and the rain will whip you with terrible gentleness and always they find you wherever you go and how can you stand in the face of all that?

Now I have a place to hide. Now I have Him to protect me.

Whshhh and shhhh and Marnie my love... Over and over He whispers to me, all day and all night He whispers to me and now I can rest here, now I'm protected here, safe in His bluebell wood.

The other one is gone now, the one that I married – I sent him away – red, red, running into the earth but no-one will find me here. I hear them calling. *Marnie! Marnie Moon!* Searching, tramping, breaking – they want to take me, to lock me away but now He protects me, now He hides me and the sky can't find me here.

Listen. Do you hear Him?

Listen. I'm safe.

I married the other one for this bluebell wood. This magical place, this protected place. This place that He put here just for me, for there are no trees on this island, there are no woods. There is only this wood.

I remember when the other one brought me to the wood. Listen, he said to me, listen, my love. Listen to the sound of the trees. Listen to the sound of the birds. And it filled me then, the sound of the wood – it snaked up inside me and filled me with its blue-green blood and I shuddered with the moist briny scent of it. It wrapped itself around my neck and it squeezed the fear from me and slithered down my throat and into the core of me.

Will you marry me, Marnie? the other one said, in the wood.

And I felt the fire that burned in my belly and I said that I would.

It was quiet at first, in the wood. Quiet; He hid from me for a while. I sat by the burn and the sun tried to find me but the sun cannot see round corners and there is no straight path through the trees into that place – He protected me even then. The sun could only brush me lightly with its fingers and He'd shake his arms and wave the sun away.

It was quiet at first, in the wood; the constant rush of water over rock like white noise wiped out the other voices.

But then I heard Him: whispering, always whispering.

He sent his messengers. A raven comes to see me sometimes; he tells me stories of the world outside. He has perched on a stone at the Ring of Brodgar; he has stood on the roofs of Skara Brae.

There's a shiny black eel who lives in the burn. On his way to the wood he broke his journey at the well at the world's end and basked in the memories of the wise old salmon who lives there still.

There are eyes in this wood but they're His eyes and so I do not fear them. The birds and the fish are His messengers but I will suffer no other creature in this wood. The other one came to find me but he is not here now. A rabbit came yesterday and ate a bluebell but then I ate the rabbit, fresh salty juices slithered down my chin and red, red, running into the earth. I tore the flesh from his bones and I threw the bones into the burn for the fish to find and

I will suffer no other creature in His wood.

Marnie Moon, loony tune.

Listen. You don't hear them now.

Margaret Elphinstone

Although I have Luddite tendencies I'm not like the narrator of my story: I live in Glasgow, I'm grateful for my laptop, I like my friends and I'm moderately capable of engaging with the contemporary world. I do, however, fantasise about living in the middle of a wood, perhaps because I spent my first ten years on the edge of a wood in Kent. I'm not naturally a city dweller, although I have lived at various times in London, Edinburgh and Glasgow. I've been involved with the women's movement, ecological and peace issues since university in the late '60s, where I read English Language and Literature. A key influence on my future writing career was the Durham University Expedition to Lapland 1970: my first encounter with true wilderness and the people who inhabit it. I began writing when living in Shetland in the 1970s, and was inspired by the landscape, the people, and the books that came my way when I worked in Shetland Library. I wrote my first novel *Islanders* when living on Papa Stour, where I also took part in my first archaeological dig. By then I had two daughters. In the 1980s we moved to Galloway where I worked as a gardener, a job that provided infinite time and space for a novelist. Time and space receded when I started work in the English Department at Strathclyde University in 1990, but other horizons expanded, as I started teaching and found new opportunities for writing. Travels in Iceland, Greenland and Canada, and two secondments to Central Michigan University were key ingredients of *The Sea Road*, *Hy Brasil* and *Voyageurs*, and a semester at the Centre for Manx Studies provided the background to *Light*. I'm now writing *And Some There Be*, a novel set on the west coast of Scotland in c6000 BC. I have two granddaughters in Galloway, where my own daughters grew up. I look forward to living in the middle of a wood again, but, unlike the narrator of my story, I want my wood to be firmly placed in contemporary Scotland.

www.margaretelphinstone.co.uk

On the Run

In the dream I'm young. I'm running from a balding man with dough-coloured skin who carries a briefcase, and a hard blonde woman. I often see the woman when I'm awake. When I had my car she used to tail-gate me on the road. She drives a massive 4x4 as big as a two-ton truck.

I used to drive a two-ton truck. I nearly lost it once when I was getting seaweed. They offered good money and they wanted the seaweed urgently. That's why, for the only time in my life, I drove along the shore on an incoming tide. I went a mile down the sand to a good place, got my pitchfork and loaded my truck with slippery-fresh weed. Then I climbed into my seat and started up. The wheels skidded in the sand. I heard them dig themselves in. I jumped out, leaving the engine running. Each wheel was sitting in a pool of water. I offloaded the seaweed and tried to start again. The wheels went round and round in pools of sea. I couldn't push and drive at the same time; I couldn't push a two ton truck anyway. I'm small, and even that huge dough-faced man with the paunch couldn't push a two-ton truck. I ran a mile back to the slipway, terrified and gasping. The truck wasn't even mine; Roddy lent it to me. I could never pay him back if I lost it. He'd never mentioned insurance. I ran and ran and prayed for a miracle.

The miracle was a man with a shiny red tractor, with a rope and tow bar, parked on the slipway. He listened to my panting plea, scratched his head, looked along the beach, shrugged his shoulders, climbed into his seat, and started up. He seemed to move so slowly! I jumped up behind him. We roared down the beach. The truck had sunk a lot further. There were pools of water all round it. Dougie fixed the rope – oh so slowly! The sea was beginning to wash around the two near wheels. Dougie kept his tractor safely up the beach, and ran the rope across. The truck strained and squelched. It came free. Dougie pulled me and my truck out of the sea just before the tide took us.

On the firm sand Dougie undid the rope, got back in his seat, and was off with a wave, cutting short my thanks. I spent all the money I had buying him a bottle of whisky. When I took it down to the village and asked where I'd find the man with the shiny red tractor they said 'Dougie? Aye, you'll find him down at the distillery. That's where he works.'

I spend a lot of time remembering these things. Sometimes it's peaceful. Sometimes it's not peaceful at all because I'm on the run.

I'm getting smaller. Everything else is getting bigger. The small grey town has swollen and burst its banks and overflowed into the water meadows. I go there as seldom as I can. People have huge cars and drive immense distances on fat sweeping roads. They build huge extensions on their houses and then live in them all alone. They eat huge meals in smart restaurants which take up more and more room in the high street. They buy huge food in gigantic supermarkets and they get hugely fat. Even their voices have grown enormous. Everything little has gone. I am little, and I am going, going, almost gone.

Small is Beautiful. I read that a long time ago.

Thinner. I'm thinner not just because I don't eat a lot now. I'm getting transparent. I look in mirrors, when I come across any, to see if the light is shining through me. I'm turning into a shadow. I have to jump off pavements so people don't walk into me. The puffy man who looks like an uncooked doughnut and the hard blonde woman know where to find me, though. They have me marked.

I know for a fact I'm marked, because they have me Disclosed. All they have to type into a computer is my name and my postcode, and then they know who I am – which is more than I do. The dough-faced man with the paunch and the hard blonde woman have my dossier on their laptops.

In this they have the advantage of me. I threw my laptop into the Leap. I did this the day I opened my emails and there were a hundred and three. I told Angie this when I met her in the Post Office. She said, 'That's nothing. I often have six hundred.' I still had the car then. I drove home, threw the laptop into the back, and tore dangerously up the winding yellow road until I got to the Leap. I parked at the top, and took the soft path down through last year's beech leaves until I was standing above the waterfall. I threw the laptop in. It vanished in a swirl of white water. I flung the cable and the mouse after it. I sat on the rock above the falls and watched all that information and communication being swept towards the sea. Everything ends up in the sea. In the sea all these small things are lost and will never be found again.

Now I'm not inundated every day by messages I don't want. No-one invites me to enlarge my penis, give my bank details or sign a petition. They've stopped offering me work. That's all right, because now that I eat less I don't need the money. They've stopped asking me out for meals or expeditions. I don't think I mind.

I always said I wanted to live in a hut in the woods. When I settled down and became normal the first thing that happened was I had to stay indoors all day. I got used to that. I sat at my desk and got fatter. My eyes hurt and I got glasses and everything came into much sharper focus than it ever had before. I did assignments and projects. I managed. The boss was a hard blonde woman and my line manager was a pasty man with a shiny face who wore boyish jeans and a tight T-shirt with his paunch overflowing his embossed leather belt. The people in the office never noticed anything odd about me. I was small but not in the least transparent, and I had my own internal strategy plan. No-one seemed to know I was an impostor. It was me that couldn't stand it any longer.

I didn't think they'd notice when I vanished. In fact they did, because even though I left no forwarding address their letters found me out. Letters from work, letters from the tax man, letters from the insurance, letters from pensions and social security, letters from the Council Tax and accountant and electoral roll, brochures and magazines from catalogues and junk mail.

Sometimes there were letters from friends, but naturally not from the dead ones. Although deep in my bones I still expect to hear from the dead people, my brain is perfectly well aware that their absence is permanent. I've not heard from Martin, for example, since I was twenty-three. We were just back from our travels. My parents had done their best to stop me hitch-hiking into the blue with a young man. They said it would be dangerous. Nothing dangerous happened except that it changed our view of the world for ever. But Martin had only been home a week when he was attacked and drowned in the Forth and

Clyde canal within a mile of his parents' house. Most people look for danger in quite the wrong places; that's one thing that hasn't changed at all.

I have seven letters from Martin. They're handwritten – the pale blue ink fading now with the passing years – unlike the streams of letters that used to pour into my post box at the foot of the track. Sometimes when I noticed the post box was overflowing I emptied it. I carried the white and brown envelopes up the hill to my hut. I sat at my table at the window, looking out at the leaves being torn off the oaks by the first gales of autumn. I'd sift through the tide of correspondence, and then drop it into the basket of kindling. I never had a newspaper to light my fire because I don't read any, but all those letters and envelopes did quite well instead (though of course I saved all the envelopes and paper that were blank on one side for my own notes – the very ones I'm writing now). Now I hardly get any letters I collect moss and birch bark and dry it above the stove. It makes much better tinder than all that paper ever did. I keep a good fire. There's plenty of dead wood around here.

I am happy here because the woods are beautiful. Just now the westering sun is slanting through the oaks. The oak tree trunks are covered with mosses, hart's tongue fern, liverworts and lichens. A tree creeper is running up and down the trunk of the oak tree by my bird table, feeding among the green and gold. The oak leaves have turned orangey-brown; the birch leaves are soft and yellow; the rowan is alive with scarlet berries. The pines, which tower over all the other trees, are dusky green that never changes. When I was a child I could climb to the top of our pine tree, using the dead dry sticks of branches like a ladder all the way up the trunk. The climb was high and airy, scary when I looked down, but once I got to the canopy the branches curled around and made a safe place: my borrowed nest where I hunkered down like a baby cuckoo and no one could get at me. The rusty pine bark was scaly-dry like a snake, and left its sticky resin smell on my grubby hands and feet.

But I digress. I am on the run. When I saw the dough-faced man again he'd grown his beard so his chins were hidden and he'd cut his hair short. He was pretending to be somebody else and I pretended not to recognise him. I hoped he'd think I wasn't me. He must have been laughing at my attempts to deceive him. The woman was there too. She'd never acknowledged me anyway. I pretended not to be me. I wanted them to think I didn't exist. I thought I'd succeeded but I was wrong. They knew all about me because I was Disclosed. I have no access to any information like that. How do I know what they've written down about me? That's why I refused to visit the doctor any more. They say you're allowed to see what they've said, but my glasses aren't strong enough now – I ignored the letters from the optician along with all the others – and I can't read the computer screen over the doctor's shoulder the way I used to do. I never cashed the prescriptions anyway. That stuff was poison. They were sucking my thoughts out of my head and dripping their ideas into me on a slow drip that kept me chained to the bed by a plastic leash. I could see my blood inside that leash – my life blood pouring away and their stuff going into me, right into my veins, without me having any chance to filter it out at all.

The Disclosure has my criminal convictions on it. It wouldn't matter now if it wasn't for the Post Office. I've cut all the other lines they have on me. But the pension I must have. I don't eat much, and some of it I gather in the woods – at this time of year all I buy some weeks is a packet of oatmeal – but there are other things: soap, matches, pens, and, most important of all, the occasional book. I love my books. They tell me what to watch for in the woods, what to gather and what to eat. They tell me how to live alone, and their kind voices take away any loneliness I might sometimes feel. For as long as my glasses last me, I'll have my books.

They traced me through the Post Office. When they closed our Post Office Sue and Jim had to shut down the shop too and after that I had to go into town every week. That's when I saw her again – behind the counter – the hard blonde woman. She stamped my book. She read my name. I knew she'd seen me. *Civil defence is common sense*. That was written up in the Post Office when I was a child. Sue and Jim were different: I could trust them. But Civil Defence ... I knew she had my Disclosure up on her computer screen with its back to me so I couldn't see it.

All this began long ago. I'd never done anything wrong, so I thought surveillance was merely a temporary inconvenience. But it was like swallowing a worm: it was very small to start with – almost invisible – but it fed on me from inside until it grew huge and bloated. The more it flourished the more I shrank. I didn't know what I was risking. They told me when I first took my car to Greenham Common – nearly thirty years ago now – that its number would be in the police computer. When I was arrested the police took my car and when I got out of prison I had to go to them and ask for it back. I drove straight to Faslane and stayed there. I was happy living in the caravan with the birch trees brushing against the roof. I like indoors to be small so the woods can hide me like a hibernating dormouse in its nest.

The first time I was arrested we were blockading Blue Gate. We sat in the road and sang *Here we sit, here we stand, here we claim our common land* ... and the shiny-faced policemen grabbed me under my arms – I was so small – and pushed me backwards. I'd have walked with them but they shoved me off my feet and they wouldn't let me walk. They threw me down and I was angry. I got up again straight away and sat back down on the tarmac. *Nuclear arms shall not command Bring the message home* ... This time when they grabbed me they threw me and I landed in a heap the breath knocked out of my body and I got up and I was so angry I sat in the road again and we sang *Carry Greenham home, ye-es, Nearer home and far away, Carry Greenham* ... And I was fighting – the frightening sweaty men – they pushed us – we were locked in the van – too many – and the waiting and the stuffiness, in the tiny cramped room all together when I was used to being out of doors under the starlight with the trees on the Common soughing in the night wind. All my life I'd had this nightmare of being locked in.

One thing I've learned in my life. I have bad dreams. I wake, gasping in relief, and I think 'Thank God, it was only a dream.' But that's just a dream itself – pure illusion. The truth about bad dreams is that they always come true. I dreamed about being locked in, and I was. Now I dream about the balding man with dough-coloured skin clutching his briefcase, and the hard blonde woman. I'm on the run. They're after me. They seize me under my arms and yank me off my feet. I wake and I listen to the wind in the trees and I think 'Thank God, it was only a dream.' But that's a lie. The true part is the dream, because all dreams come true.

And we did have a dream. *I have a dream* … I don't need a book for that; I don't need glasses to see those words up close. It's far away now and I remember every word. It kept me going. That's how I got my Record. I kept on going in spite of being locked in. I didn't realise I wasn't free. I didn't know I couldn't just walk away whenever I chose. I look at people looking at their computers and reading about me while I read their faces and I realise I can never run far enough because I'm one of the Disclosed. I'm on the run.

It won't be long now. While I'm writing this the pasty-faced man and the hard blonde woman are on their way. You can't hide in the woods because they can always find you, however far away they are. They see your blood pulsing through your veins – you're a little red puddle on a surveillance screen, and even if you wriggle into thickets of bramble and honeysuckle, or lie down in deep bracken, or crawl into the hollow of an old oak, they can see you from as far away as they like, from outside the earth if that suits them, just like God. They know exactly where to find me.

When they come to my door I'm ready. I climb out of the rooflight and leap to the ground. I stumble through wet leaves, dodging mossy rocks and rotting wood. I trip over tussocks and squelch through cotton grass. I'm under the beech trees, tearing dangerously downhill towards the Leap. The man who made that Leap was running from the Hanoverian soldiers – nearly three hundred years ago now – and he got away. He was a big strong man like Dougie who saved me with his shiny red tractor. I can't make that leap. I'm small. If I try I'll land in the waterfall, and be lost in a swirl of white water. I'll be swept out to sea, and they'll never be able to find me there.

I'm running over the slippery rocks above the Leap. Someone swerves into my path. It's Dougie. He's as fierce and strong as the enormous lumpen man with the briefcase. There's a young woman with Dougie. She's very small. She looks like Martin. The hard blonde woman grabs the young woman, knocking me off balance. I'm falling. The small woman who looks like Martin has a jam jar. She throws whatever's in it into the hard blonde woman's face. The woman's face dissolves. Acid. That was acid. I hate her but I'm sorry for her. Her face is a smooth brown mask and her eyes have gone. And Dougie is fighting the dough-faced man whose chins glisten like lard as he lashes out at Dougie's throat. Now he's taken his gun out of his briefcase and he's holding it at Dougie's head but Dougie has a gun too and he's pressing it against the cruel man's overflowing belly like sticking a pencil into a cushion. I don't know who will win. The Leap is right behind me but I'm small. Dougie could jump across. Dougie is strong like the clansman who fled from the soldiers but I'm not. I can't jump that far. All I can do is leap in and the waterfall swallows me and sweeps me out to sea and now they can never catch me or find any trace of me again and I am free.

That didn't happen. Obviously not, or I wouldn't be sitting here in my hut in the woods writing this. I'm alive. My glasses are perched on the end of my nose, so when I look up I can see over them. A siskin and two blue tits are pecking away at the peanuts that hang from the oak tree. There's a thrush singing in the rowan. The sun casts its last rays slantwise, turning the green of the wood to gold. It's tea time. Today I gathered field mushrooms, a puffball and three chanterelles, and I still have two eggs from the half-dozen I bought from Angie, and a smidgen of fresh milk. I could make a mushroom omelette and have a cup of tea. That part I wrote just now – that was the dream.

Meg Bateman

My poem below can serve as an introduction to myself. I was advised not to include it in my last collection, *Soirbheas/Fair Wind,* because its voice was more ironic than the rest. However, it expresses something I often feel: an impatience with things I think are unimportant and a simultaneous longing to be more engaged with them. Ultimately I upbraid myself for this position because life is made up of just such inconsequential goals, and which one of us can say what an appropriate ambition for life should be?

I have always needed a creative outlet, which varies between music, painting and writing. I am very gratified that there are those who are willing to publish and read what I have to say. I would go mad if I did not have this outlet to express things as they are, without political, religious or social spin.

I was born in Edinburgh of largely English parents and consider myself a first-generation Scot. I learnt Gaelic out of curiosity about another culture co-existing with English in Scotland. I have found my poetic voice through Gaelic and its literature, but am presently trying a new medium, English. Most of my energies are taken up with teaching and research at Sabhal Mòr Ostaig in Skye. I have brought out three collections of poetry and have co-edited and translated four anthologies of medieval, 17th century, religious and women's Gaelic verse. I live with my son and a few animals, and have a partner fifty miles away. He says that is the best we can manage.

A' Bheatha na Rìomhachas Suarach

Tha farmad agam ris an tè
a ruitheas a-steach do bhuth-thìodhlac
air na làithean saora aice
is a thig a-mach làn toilichte
le àilleagan beag air choreigin;

Agus ris an tè a thadhlas air Marks and Spencers
air a rathad dhachaigh
agus le àilgheas nach beag, a ghlacas
"blas brìoghmhor na h-Eadailt",
"an rud mu dheireadh às an Fhraing";

Agus ris an eòlaiche, amhach
a' taomadh thar na lèine
a dh'iarnaig a bhean, 's e a' cur dheth
às a chathair leathair,
casan beaga biorach a' stiùireadh ri Nèamh…

Ged tha magadh an cuid pròis
an lùib an fharmaid, b' fheàrr leam
gu robh an aon chridhealas agams'
dhan a' bheatha a' dannsadh air oir an rathaid
na rìomhachas suarach, 's sinne greasad seachad.

Life in her Glad-Rags

I envy the woman
who can pop into a gift shop
on her holidays
and come out delighted
with some trinket,

or who can visit Marks and Spencer's
on the way home
and through her discernment, capture
the "genuine taste of Italy,"
the "ultimate from France."

And I envy the expert, who
with neck bulging over the shirt
ironed by the wife,
pronounces from his leather chair,
small feet protruding heavenwards...

Though in my envy I may sneer
at their pride, I wish I shared
their affection
for life dancing in her glad-rags
at the roadside as we hurry past.

Morag MacInnes

I was born and brought up in Stromness, in Orkney. Spent four years pretty much tongue-tied at Edinburgh University, because the other tutorial members were older taller thinner blonder and Englisher than me. Then went to Shetland, during the oil boom. Vast influx of folk, rapid change – many different voices (most still taller and thinner than me). Had children with a Glasgow man, who writes about urban life, tenement stories – another strange voice. Went to Germany; lived in a tower block outside Cologne with Turkish folk, Italians, poor white Germans – and a man with a limp that he got in World War 2 fighting us. When local kids came to ask if my girls wanted to go out to play, I couldn't understand them. I was tongue-tied regularly in supermarkets. I learned what dispossession was like; voicelessness. Moved to Lincolnshire, trying always to get back to Orkney but never getting a job. Discovered that a Scots accent gives you a spurious kudos, in some bits of England. Also, conversely, that having an English accent gave folk kudos in Scotland.

Finally returned home, to discover a very changed place. The dialects are all different again, a mixter maxter.

My experiences have meant that I'm fascinated by what on earth a voice is – let alone a Scottish voice – and problems of identity keep reappearing in my work. I also live opposite Skara Brae, the World Heritage site run by Historic Scotland, which means I can count the number of buses which pour in daily. This leads to more ruminations about what Scotland is, what history is, what language is and whether you should try to preserve ideas about nationhood like flies in amber or whether you should embrace the increasing diversity of the world.

As for being a woman writing here and now – it's fun! Orkney's writing scene is buoyant; Two Ravens Press has helped, as has the George Mackay Brown Fellowship, to give us a sense of confidence. The communication between island groups has improved mightily – Shetland, Orkney and the Western isles have lots to teach each other.

The Direction of One's Gaze

Christ but he was tired. Too many displays. If it's Tuesday it must be Belgium, or the East of England bloody cattle show or some Jock Highland Games.

Air looks the same no matter what country you're in. Cloud cover is cloud cover. The aircraft's manoeuvres are the same too, the space you take up and the space you leave between you and the rest of the team. It's perfectly worked out, no room for error, you just lock on. But Christ, he was tired.

Nothing against the Jocks. A sort of Jock himself, the right sort, the sort the RAF likes. Cut his teeth in Gordonstoun, wears a kilt to weddings, that sort of Jock. Wouldn't actually live there, but it's in the blood. No, nothing against Bonnie Scotland, just that he could have done without another show back-to-back with the Cologne extravaganza. Look on the bright side, it's a tiny island gala, no need to go the whole hog, a few flyovers will be fine.

You just lock on and concentrate, eyes on the leader, don't think.

It always took him time to adjust, after a tour. It was hard to re-focus, people shifted more dramatically than flight instruments and he couldn't always compensate. Days would go by when he couldn't get her and the kid into his sightlines. He didn't notice it that much but she did. Made a joke of it. We all sit round looking in different directions, she said, it's like being in an art gallery.

She was interested in that sort of thing. Officers' wives wouldn't have been seen dead with a pay-check when he first joined, but it's different now. She did a course, writes exhibition brochures and so on. It's made her flashier, mixing with culture. Dinky little racy car, sharp suits and a briefcase, he likes that.

It gives her funny ideas. No – it gives her ideas he doesn't know enough about to know whether they're funny ha ha, funny peculiar or just plain wrong.

If it had been music that would have been different, he knew the score, hah, that's a goodun.

No point in fretting, get the show over then think about the email.

In the Mess they were talking about some astronaut with tinnitus. He wouldn't have an op because he was a Christian Scientist, suffered for bloody years, gave in, had surgery and wouldn't you know it, God wasn't mocked. Took away the buzz and left him with a noise like bells chiming. Tinnitus, the pilot's nightmare, eternal bells of hell night after night, deafness would be better than that.

Funny how they all got religion – didn't John Glenn too? Something to do with seeing the earth from Up There and wanting it to be looked after. You can feel sorry for anything if you're far enough away. If it's small enough to take in in one glance. Up close is different; he left all that to Penny. She did up close. She said to him: when you meet people all you care about is what car they drive.

Yes, he said, why not?

No good. He moved to the window with a hot sweet coffee, unfolded the printout.

> *Re: wimmelbilder*
> *Look it up, I am definitely gone this time, wont be back, blame landscape with fall of icarus Penny*

It was routed from Brussels, early, 6.18am.

– All right, Jon?

Blackie Blackwell at his elbow.

– Yeah, fine. Is it a goer?

– Rain and low cloud, dunno yet. Do our best for them though, nice little occasion. Lovely place, Dad was there, in the Flow, in the war. Great fishing, bloody awful weather.

– I'll get my head down for half an hour, I think.

Brewer's Phrase and Fable in the bookshelf – they were all dictionary freaks, crossword addicts, part of the honourable tradition. Used to be waiting for war, now it's waiting for gala weather. Hey ho. Icarus.

Nothing there he didn't know. Flew with his father from Crete, sun melted the wax and he fell into the sea, blah de blah.

If this email had come five years ago it would have meant it's over because I can't stand the strain, I'm afraid you'll die and leave us alone. It couldn't be that now. She barely noticed when he went off. She was often away herself. The boy turned out like him in the end – he was like her till school, which sorted him out, thank God. He was good at physics and chess and didn't make a fuss.

What the hell was she doing in Brussels? Had she told him and he'd forgotten?

She'd been scared of flying ever since she was a kid. She'd been with the family, high summer beach, donkeys and so on, and some smart cookie decided to do a bit of low flying over the castle, couldn't recover from the dive and fell into the sea in front of a thousand happy campers. She said it went quiet for a minute and you could hear the fuselage fizzing. Then the kids went back to playing. If I'd blinked I'd've missed it, but I didn't, she said. Up one minute, dead the next.

Shouldn't happen, he'd said. Misjudgements or mechanical failure make crashes and both are absolutely avoidable if you are scientific about things.

I'll have to work on that, she said. Rationalising risk factors.

He pointed out that she hadn't got the right kind of mind. Just after that they'd been on the motorway and he'd hit a badger, a great bloody black thing, and they'd had an argument about the Highway Code and she went awol for the first time. Because she thought he could have avoided the badger.

Maybe I could have, he said, once she was safely back. I could have swerved, but if I had I shouldn't have, you silly cow. You weigh up the risks, and it was us or some rodent.

Best view ever was the Greek islands. Mountains are always good, snow in sunset, any coastline with a frothy edge. I can cut the world down to size, Meccano towns, Noah's Ark countryside. But you get used to seeing the world from high up, in miniature. You stop noticing.

In the end it was a predictable little run: nice little grey Scotchy town. Perfect stone circle, like a message. An e mail to God. Oi, look at us, we think You're great, look at this picture we made You. Squads of happy Jocks swilling malt afterwards, talking about war and oil. Good to get home and he expected her to be there twisting her feet like a bad kid. He never had more than bits of her in his mind's eye, earring against slice of jaw, zipped hip.

The place was empty. No food in the fridge. Another man? Bloody inconceivable. Check her mail. The phone bill. The credit cards.

It is much smaller and brighter than she had imagined. She feels like an astronaut looking at earth and seeing a precious, precious jewel on a black velvet cloth. Icarus is in Greece, she knows, because she recognises the azure colour. He has been with the Gods, out of his own element. The sky rears above marble mountains.

She peers. The attendant isn't alarmed. She has been in the Musée des Beaux Arts every day for a week, and she doesn't pose a threat to the painting. You get a lot of Breughel obsessives. They're harmless.

At the very top of the picture the colour heats up, hot enough, of course, to melt wax. The shepherd cranes his neck, searching for a break in the weather. The dog's listless, letting the lead dangle. The fisherman's beer mug is empty. The horse plods towards shade. How good it would be, she thinks, if they could tear off those thick Dutch sacks they're trussed up in, and dive into the sea. Because there is a wind on the sea, a brisk cool breeze, you can tell by the sails. Only one bather. His legs writhe, disturbing the gulls. Poor Icarus.

What did he think, she wonders. Did he think: this is what comes of pride? Or maybe: so this is where science gets you, the sorry result of misjudgement and mechanical failure – me with my undignified little legs threshing the air? Whatever the answer, here he is, drowning forever in a Brussels gallery.

– I feel so sorry, she says to the attendant, for Icarus.

– He didn't listen, he had to push a little bit too high, said the attendant. His English was excellent but the intonation was all wrong, and she was reminded of how very high and far she had flown.

– Nobody's helping him, she insisted, pointing at the lumpish shepherd. Everyone's looking the wrong way, like Auden said in the poem.

– You act stupid, the world punishes you, said the attendant. I loved *Four Weddings*, didn't you?

– Not that poem. The one where the ship has somewhere to go. This picture, it's about.

Later, with Herringsalat and beer, she took out the catalogue, found the Landscape again. He would have been a horrible young man, sure he was right, arrogant, self-obsessed. But there should always be someone to help. Again she found the man halfway up the rigging. Perhaps he's shouting Man Overboard, she thought. Or perhaps that fisherman bloke isn't casting his rod, but throwing an arm out. I'll go back tomorrow and just check. It'll make me feel better.

She told him she was leaving a hundred times. He never heard. She even practised leaving, to give him a chance to call up the fisherman and the men on the rigging, get them apprised of the situation so he wouldn't drown. But he didn't get the picture. He looked the other way.

He found it in her *Art Reader*. Wimmelbilt. A teeming figure picture. Masses of small figures presented on a large painting surface seen from above, as in Breughel's *Children's Games*. Containing general truths about the human condition, rather than individualised portraits. Perhaps less profound, because of the allegorical, formalised nature of the representation.

Balancing Equations

Everybody said he wasna all there. But they didna have fancy words for whit might be wrong. He wasna stupid, that's for sure. He could do logarithms withoot the book. Betty knew it wasna stupidness, it was something missan in his cleverness. A want, she said, the bairn's got a want.

She was at the Fisherman's Society all day guttan, she was some filleter, due to bean disappointed in love. She whupped the vitals oot o that poor damn fish as if they were Sigurd, her first, Puddock her second, or Bjorn, who had just recently returned to the gentler attentions o his ma in Stavanger.

All day she ripped and tossed guts. At night, tenderly, she rowed herring in oatmeal as if she wis beddin a baby. No chance o wan o them though, no more bairns. Just them two. The salty fryan smell rose and tormented the cats. She and he ate wi them twinan roond their ankles.

If it was fair, they went oot so he could coont things, up Brinkies or on the new golf course. Wet meant jigsaws. Shopping Week wis a mixed blessing. Plenty to coont, but he went awful excited and daft-like, she had to keep an eye.

He liked twos and fours and sixes but no threes. Liked the egg timer for its eight shape, an fur another reason to do wi the way the sand slipped centrally through the cone o itsel. The interlappan rectangles of red cream and blue on the lino pleased him. The rise o the school windows wis good as weel; the science room had six, subdivided into twelves. When they were open, the bisecting lines o sash, pane, curtain an hooky pole made his heart beat fast.

If there wis equations left on the blackboard, he wanted to touch them, fur their balance.

If the moon looked in on him at night, all by itsel wanan in the big sky and worryan him, he would think: for every action there is an equal and opposite reaction. It helped him sleep.

English wis hard; nothing stayed tidy. You hid to blame the adjectives, subject verb and object fine, but throw in that adjectives? Anything could happen. Words slipped doon the cone of theresels and came oot different. He got nothing oot o ten every time. The teacher measured his verticals wi a ruler. They were never straight except in his head, where the angles wis regular as soldiers. But in number work there'd be red pencil ticks all doon the Orkney Education Committee ink exercise book, the wan wi the magical mantras printed on the back, roods an perches an poles.

He saw that Mr Ferguson wis an angry kind o man. He kent why. Nobody in his class could see the patterns the numbers made, (the nine times table bonny as a snowflake) – nobody but him, an there wis no point in teachan him, he wouldna be goan fur a Bursary to get to Aberdeen and mak a teacher prood. His writing wis like the tail a snail maks crossan concrete. He just kent every maths class made Mr Ferguson sad, then cross because the only bairn wi half an idea wis wantan.

Mostly mam wasna there, but she wis always just coman, so that wis all right. He could set the fire an peel tatties , use the beak o the tin opener to mak two neat triangles in the Carnation Milk tin so it would pour right on the fruit salad.

Sometimes there wis a man aboot but no fur long. The baker's boy cam early in the mornin fur a while wi the softies still warm, sausage rolls that fell off his tray. He didna like him because o the black hairs thrustan up through the laces o his floory plimmers, that laces no tied up right either. The coalie wis the opposite, the whitest nails whar he chewed them. There wis a man fae Aberdeen that travelled wi big books o wallpaper. That wis better, you could shut yur eyes and rub the raised patterns and then open ur eyes, see if you'd read them right.

When Mr Ferguson started coming it was different. Mam pit her fags ahint the clock. They all had tea, Gipsy Creams, he wasna sent through and told to knock on the wall if he wanted anything. Instead Mr Ferguson did geometry wi him. Every time he got it right the teacher would say, 'That's remarkable, boy,' an shak his head at Mam.

He'd sat ootside the hairdresser, heard her under the drier, shoutan aboot him, he'd heard Stanley and Toots next door saying you poor sowl, whit an affliction, is there no a place you can send him like Cornhill?, he'd laid on the OFS pier throwan crab shells at the lasses and heard her gabban on her break: there things he does would drive a man wild, no man wid pit up wi it, that's how I'm where I am noo.

He wouldna go to the toilet, no fur days; when he felt it coman he would lean on the wall and clench himsel up. He would bring stones in, mak patterns then step ower an roond them all night, ower an roond, ower an roond. He sang, 'there's a tiny house, on a tiny stream, where a lovely lass had a lovely dream.' An echo song, ower an ower.

It drove mam wild but he just had to do these things, they had to be started and gone through and feenished to keep the balance right. Otherwise it wis a half-done sum. Who could sleep wi a sum half done?

He kent it wis hard on her havan to pit his sausages the right way roond the clapshot, keep the towel straight on the roller, the bathmat parallel to the bath. She wisna a tidy number. But she always came into bed wi him if it thundered or the maroons went off, an they always cuddled up under the quilt wi the stitching he liked to trace, to watch the fireworks on the last night o Shopping Week.

'An you a big boy fur goodness' sake,' she said. But did it.

There wis a lot aboot gala week that sent him into his coontin games. Folk behaved different, dressed in disguises. The penny games at the Showies were rigged, the darts weighted wrongly, you couldna nail the Queen atween her gimlet eyes fur love nor money. The last night Saturday fireworks made up fur all that. The bursting oot bothered him, he held on hard to mam, but then – fur every action! You saw it work – rockets, starbursts, cascades, if you screwed yur eyes up there wis hundreds o crosses drawn in light in the sky, reflected in the water, doubled, doubled, hundreds an hundreds o doubles echoing each other ower an under, an the noise doubled too, booman back fae Brinkies. Mam went to the Open Air Dance on the pier every year but she always came back on time, he would hear her hing her coat on the hook, tak her stilettos off. Then she brought up a bottle o Mowatt's lemonade an Rich Tea biscuits sandwiched thegither wi jam. They wrapped up, shiny green quilt, parallel stitching, her smell – fags, powder, Evening in Paris, on top o the fish guts.

She would say, I wonder whit'll be first, white or green or red? Every time she was wrong. She just laughed. She jumped at every bang like he did, an said, my Godfathers whit a shock. He would laugh and laugh, nearly choke wi delight, an shout, but you ken it'll bang once it's up in the air, it's no a shock at all!

It is to your poor daft mammy, she said then, an hugged him hard. Every year, they said that an she hugged him hard.

Soppan grey rain, midgies hingin ower the water in clouds. Mr Ferguson had been cumman wi more puzzles an he never mentioned vertical handwriting. He wis maybe a friend.

I see numbers like colours, Mr Ferguson, he said, fur a test. I can see inside o a triangle too. Hid's's red. But a square is blue. Hid's dependable.

Mr Ferguson didna laugh or look, he brought a record and said, listen to the patterns on this, and went ben to mam's tea an Gypsy Creams.

Ower an ower, he played it, till the equations made sense. He nivver knocked on the wall all night.

That's a man called Mozart, said Mr Ferguson. He wis gettan a kipper fur his breakfast, a fat one.

Jimmy Young's better, said mam. Unchained Melody.

Him an Mr Ferguson looked at each other, like pals do. She didna understand.

Saturday night mam wis twitchy. She rolled up her front hair in rollers, ironed her dress. He started pelletin his bread because she wis odd. Then she said it.

What would you think if Mr Ferguson watched the fireworks wi us this year?

In wur quilt? he thought. No snuggled up, that would be silly.

He said: he wouldna want to do a thing like that.

Why no?

He's me teachur!

She breathed oot, pit the iron up, lit a fag.

He said he would like it, fur it's an awful good view.

No, he shouted, it wouldna be because o that at all. It would be anither reason.

Whit other reason? she said, going red as the ironed dress on the board. You nasty-minded peedie so-an-so, his somebody been yappin at the school to you about him and me? Folk hiv no idea what I put up wi in this hoose, it's no as if I don't deserve some humankindness.

No, he said, nearly cryan which wis the worst o all upsets and took weeks o coontin, dividin an stone walkin to sort. I mean, he would want to come fur the patterns, no for the view, that's a lie, mammy. He would WANT to come but he wouldna, mammy

Why would he no? You're havering, beuy, I shoulda kent you'd hiv some mad notion. And will you leave me bread BE.

She wis a mean triangle o eyes and mouth, all pointy.

I'm that sick o your nonsense. Whit way would he no come?

He wis scared to say numbers to her. It wis like the Mozart music thing. But oot it came.

Because o the balance. Hid's a three!

She pit the loaf back in the bin and swept all his rolled grey bits, twenty o them, very fast into her ither hand, and went oot the back to hurl them at the gulls. She wis away a while. When she came back she said,

Weel that's fine. I just wondered. I'll no forget wur lemonade.

Pauline Prior-Pitt

I was born in Hull, enjoy being a Yorkshire woman and am grateful to have inherited the genes of one Irish grandfather. In other lives, I was an actress, teacher, special needs adviser, and mother to three children, now well grown.

In June 1997 my husband Robert and I came on a three-week holiday to the Isle of North Uist. Although we had been to Scotland many times, we hadn't visited these islands before. By the end of our second week we began to look for a house. At the end of our third week we found an old croft house with the sea at the bottom of the field. In June 1998 we moved in. I had always lived in towns and cities but somewhere inside my head I recognised this place.

The sea drew me here, and the silence, the safety, the sense of community. Walking the long silver beaches, close to the waves is about as good as it gets for me. And swimming in the sea; I need that.

My writing has changed. I write about women's issues; our juggling lives; didn't think I would want to write about the island, but slowly the landscape seeps into my poems.

The poetry scene appears to be closer in Scotland: everyone seems to know about everyone else, but living in such a remote area I don't often meet other poets or get to their readings. However, I have access through the internet, and people find me on my website. The Scottish Poetry Library, Scottish Pamphlet Poetry and Poetry Scotland are lifelines. Gradually, an audience for my work in Scotland is building: winning the Callum Macdonald Award certainly helped, but many of my performances are at festivals and events in England.

Other than writing; I paint quite seriously; organise monthly poetry evenings during the winter; run a writing group, attend Tai Chi classes and Pilates classes. I chair a group bringing complementary therapists over to the island. And I go for long walks on the shore.

www.pauline-prior-pitt.com

Pauline Prior-Pitt

Deep

From rock pools, wet, delicious
I held your precious pebbles

kept them wet, like jewels
in my mouth, slipped them

our secrets, under my skin.

Now they are dull, dry,
and weighing the secret places

clustered too deep
to set down on the shore for you to see.

"CRUMBS!"

It would seem that men
have a different relationship to crumbs.
They like to see them on the breadboard
with a fair scattering across the surfaces.

They seem to need crumbs to be there.
Even when you clear them,
clean every one off the board,
wipe every surface before you leave,

on your return, they will be there;
crumbs all over again
with maybe even a buttery knife
and a jar of marmite with its lid off.

You wonder if this is supposed to be a piece of art,
an installation based on still life:
"crumbs scattered on board
with unlidded marmite and buttery knife".

Maybe you are frustrating his artistic talent
constantly wiping away his attempts
This could be a work in progress, to be left
day after day, for weeks, months until it is complete,

when it can be moved, on a day without wind,
into The Gallery of Modern Art,
displayed with his artist's statement
about waste, poverty and frustration.

Who knows what might happen?
If he was feeling hungry at the time
and fancied, a simple meal of bread, butter and marmite
maybe Charles Saatchi would buy it.

But of course, men don't say
and until they do
you carry on
wiping all their crumbs away.

Gone

She is winter now.
Her gaze shrunk to a window pane.

Dead grass torn from tussocks
scatters to the fence.

Rain veils blot out distant hills.
Sea and sky dissolve into the same grey.

Wild geese, in loose formation,
cry, " gone, gone, gone."

Pauline Prior-Pitt

The Uncovering

She took a sledgehammer
to the coal store
by the back door.

Broke ugly concrete-blocks
into hard core,
then slice by slice removed rough turf.

And digging deep
filled forty barrow loads
with earth and stones

scraping and scouring
the last remaining soil,
brushing away fine dust

until the rock appeared.
A steady downpour washed it clean.
And here it is.

Outcrop of gneiss,
solid cream grey swirling rock,
rust patched in places

laminated with rich quartz ,
striated in deep grooves
where ancient ice crushed past.

A hollow in the rock
has filled with rain
to make a bath for sparrows.

And in sharp crevices
white pebbles look like waterfalls.

Pauline Prior-Pitt

Trapped

As if trapped
inside her head

their wings
tangled

in the net
of her brain

fluttering
in her tight throat

filling her mouth
with feathers;

words
struggle to escape

when making
the smallest sound

is too much
to ask.

Regi Claire

My coming to Scotland is down to chance, really – and love. I'm Swiss by birth and upbringing. English is my fourth language. While a student of German and English at Zurich University, I was awarded one of two annual exchange scholarships with Britain, both at Aberdeen University. A few years later, my then partner chose to do his final thesis about the Scottish author Ron Butlin…

The rest is history: Ron and I got married in 1993, and I and my golden retriever moved to Edinburgh. Although working on a PhD on Graham Swift at the time, I'd always felt more drawn to imaginative writing, but never dared. With Ron's encouragement, I did. And, when I found I could get published and even win a competition (Edinburgh Review 10th Anniversary Short Story Competition), I gladly gave up the PhD.

My first collection of stories, *Inside~Outside,* was shortlisted for the Saltire First Book Award, and my first novel, *The Beauty Room*, was longlisted for the Allen Lane/MIND Book of the Year Award. My work has been widely published in anthologies and literary magazines in Britain and abroad as well as broadcast on Radio 4. I've received bursaries from SAC, Pro Helvetia and Thurgau Lottery Foundation as well as a UBS Cultural Foundation Award.

Living in a country I didn't grow up in and writing in a language that isn't my mother tongue has made me keenly aware of my 'in-between-ness'. It's a force field I try to explore creatively by giving voice to people who don't quite belong. Often, these outsiders are shown at crisis point. They may feel misunderstood or manipulated, or turn into predators. What I hope shines through, though, is a plea for acceptance and compassion, if not love.

Regi Claire

Invisible Partners

Towards dusk I often go and sit in the church. A walk along windswept pavements with slabs so uneven I have to lift my feet up high. Like wading on solid ground. Once I fell and hurt my knee and now whenever I try to hurry, the pain is like a brake pad cutting through my joint.

I am fond of this church. Its simplicity is so different from the baroque excesses I was used to as a child, decades ago, in my own country. There are no knick-knacks here, just glass and stone and wood. A heraldic ceiling and pews of pitch pine, stone pillars without carvings, a stone arch with three stained-glass windows and, to the left, several dark shadows like sweat marks in the shape of something. People say it's a ghost. Sometimes, they say, you can see its heart beating; then the wall begins to vibrate and there are flickers of light and harsh scraping noises like the grinding of millstones.

How I have prayed to catch a glimpse of that ghost! Just for the sake of action, and a flare of life beyond the grave. Not that I'm particularly religious. Our wedding ceremony over, Jim didn't leave me much leisure to commune with God – or with myself, for that matter – between getting me pregnant and installing me behind the counter of his grocer's shop.

Now, of course, they're all long gone: the children, Jim, the generations of mice in the storeroom and the cats that chased them.

Late last night the phone rang, the first time since my birthday at the weekend. Static, screeches and howls greeted me and I knew at once it was Michael, intrepid wanderer, photojournalist and heartbreaker.

'Sorry about the racket, Mum,' he cried. 'I'm in the middle of the Amazon rainforest. How are you?'

'Son, good to hear from you. I thought you'd forgotten me.' A half-laugh. Truth was, he had forgotten my birthday. (Unlike his younger twin sisters with their dutiful calls from Zurich and Geneva, their flowers, chocolates and family snaps.) 'Trust me, Michael,' I added, my laughter a little more grating now, 'I'm as fine as I shall ev–'

Another screech, sounding much closer.

'Wow, that was a blue-and-yellow macaw! Beautiful birds, Mum, you'd love them!'

Michael's enthusiasm was genuine – genuinely juvenile in a man of forty-six.

I told him I'd seen a macaw before. At the zoo. Much safer for everyone concerned, wouldn't he say?

I'd not changed one bit, he exclaimed. 'Still your pugnacious old self!'

Against a background of ear-piercing shrieks, I asked when he'd be back in Scotland.

'Next summer, probably. Got some unfinished business.'

No need to inquire any further. Wherever he went, Michael's path was littered with broken hearts. Not for the first time I found myself wondering whether, in addition to my five carefully accounted-for Swiss grandchildren, there were others scattered across the globe, nameless and of all colours, ages and religions, with my son's grey eyes. That's when the static on the line grew suddenly unbearable.

The leaves in the churchyard scrunch under my feet and I imagine the dead whispering among themselves as they feel me passing above.

Seventy-one, seventy-one, seventy-one, they're saying, *quite a few years yet until she joins us.*

I thrust my head out and push into the breeze with deliberate exaggeration, letting my coat tails flap wildly as I show off my new navy blue shoes with the velcro-fasteners (my own birthday treat to myself). Halfway to the church porch I have to stop for a moment to regain my breath, one hand on a gravestone for support. After all, I don't intend to arrive within those spectral walls puffing like an ancient locomotive. The walk has tired me rather more than usual; my back is aching and my knee about to seize up.

'Regular exercise won't do you any harm, Rosa, provided you take it easy,' my GP said only last week, writing out the new prescription for my painkillers.

'You know I'm a tough old bird, Doctor,' I replied with a resonant laugh – though perhaps it was merely a loud cackle, the cackle of a silly old bird.

Now, leaning harder on the gravestone, I repeat, 'Silly old bird, silly old bird.'

Around me the afternoon is all blue and tarnished gold, and I ignore the drunken shouts from a nearby pub.

I've always been a bit of a talker, to be honest. At the shop this was an asset; most of the customers liked a few minutes' chit-chat or gossip, especially if it came in a lilting foreign accent. At home Jim used to complain, saying I was worse than the radio – no off-button. After his death I carried on talking, in a mish-mash of Swiss German and English, to all the empty rooms in the flat, sometimes even to the woman in the mirror, watching the lines in her face deepen and her hair turn silver. It gives me a thrill to feel my lips and tongue moving, slowly or rapidly, depending on my mood, and the bursts of air from my mouth prove I'm still alive.

My fingers have begun to trace the badly eroded surface of the gravestone, along the crumbling grooves of some letters. 'RIP,' I hear myself murmur. 'Whoever you are.'

There's a sharp rustle to my right and the black-and-white flash of a single magpie as it flies up into one of the sycamores. Chattering angrily, it starts crashing about the foliage.

'Rosie! No! Don't!' A woman's voice.

I jerk round. Not many people call me Rosie here, only a few friends from the Swiss Club and Gary and Stephen, my neighbours.

At first I can't see anyone. Then I notice a bow-legged bull terrier doing its business next to a marble gravestone. Slowly it angles its head to stare over at me from small pig eyes. The metal spikes on its collar glint in the low slanting rays of the sun. Taking my chance, I sidle off, with vague pacifying gestures, towards the safety of the church.

Leaves, broken twigs and feathers drift down from the sycamore, chased by shrill bird cries.

'Sorry!' A young woman has appeared at my elbow. She is as pale as death and there are two silver rings in her nostrils. 'I didn't mean to disturb you. Rosie can be such a naughty wee thing.' She smiles indulgently, then bends to pat the dog that has ambled up to her, its fat pink tongue lolling like a bacon rasher.

For a moment I am reminded of myself, years ago, holding little Michael's hand and popping a peppermint cream into his mouth as I apologise yet again for one of his pranks. When the girl straightens up, my hand is curled around empty air.

'That's okay,' I say. 'I thought you meant me, you see.'

'Pardon?' The girl's lips are painted an odd shade of purplish black and her short-cropped hair has the look of wet tar. She isn't naturally pale, I realise now and quickly glance away, mumbling, 'Well, I'm also…'

But she is already walking off. 'I'd better pick that up,' she calls over her shoulder.

The bull terrier sniffs my new shoes, from toes to heels and back again, before nosing along the tails of my raincoat.

I stand rigid, try counting to ten. *Four, five, six* –

The bald, pink snout nudges my left shin.

I smile down at it uneasily. A nasty-looking animal. 'Good dog,' I quaver, avoiding the pig eyes.

The snout inspects my other shin, releasing hot meaty exhalations up the inside of my leg.

'Shoo now, shoo,' I mutter and set off casually, pretending to stroll rather than run-and-stall towards the church porch; the bull terrier trots by my side, panting.

'Rosie?'

The dog stops at once and so do I, quite instinctively.

'Rosie! Here!' The girl has vanished among the gravestones and briars.

Swivelling its head in my direction every few steps, the dog finally slinks off and I sigh with relief, then continue my way up onto the porch.

As I reach for the brass door handle into my sanctuary, I become aware again of the drunken shouts from before. They sound louder now, nearer – and that's when I catch sight of a group of young people gathered at the bottom of the churchyard in the late afternoon sun. Dressed in black like mourners, with mops of green, orange and blue hair, they're lounging on the tombs, smoking and gulping from big plastic cider bottles. Three girls have started a chant-and-dance around a Celtic cross. Like straggly crows they flap their arms, skip, lurch and strut. Now some of the men give chase while the others cheer them on with yells and wolf-whistles and the bull terrier barks excitedly. One girl ends up getting brandished about in the air, pummelling her assailant's black leather jacket, kicking and squealing. The rest of them shriek and howl. Friends indeed!

I brace myself, ready to make a limping rush towards the girl with the words, *I'll help you if no one else will!* – when I see her being laid down on a tomb behind some bushes and, perfectly quiet and docile now, pulling up her T-shirt to let Leather Jacket fondle her breasts.

Suddenly, the shouts and screams and giggles are more than I can take. Much more. Worse than the din of Michael's rain-forest.

There's no one else in the church. Only me, the wooden pews, the stained glass with its fading images of the Crucifixion on the stone floor. And the marks on the wall. I sit down in the front row and try to concentrate on them. But it's hard to shut out the noise from the churchyard. I want to see the ghost. I must see it. Now.

'NOW! NOW! NOW!'

The loud viciousness of my voice makes me jump. I clap a hand to my mouth and slip the scarf over my ears. All at once flitting shadows begin to weave across the windows outside. Dizzy, I gaze up at the heraldic ceiling. Straight above me is a perfectly carved red heart. *I am a sane person*, I tell myself, *I don't need ghosts*.

Just then there's a gust of wind that tugs my scarf loose. The heavy door falls into the lock with a bump. Footsteps and low murmurings. I ignore them. *Real* worshippers, probably, praying in muted tones.

Suddenly, hysterical laughter fills the nave. 'See the ghost? It's bloody moving!'

'Hey, pipe down.'

'No shit, Geoff, it *is* moving! Look!'

'Forget about it, okay.' A pause, followed by a creak. 'There now. That's better, isn't it?'

But *I* still can't see anything. No vibrations. No flickers of light. Nothing. NOTHING. The same old marks cover the same old patches of wall. And the scraping noises, clearly those of wood on stone, come from the back of the church.

I get to my feet abruptly and stumble towards the door.

Their black-clad bodies are almost indistinguishable from the pitch pine of the pew on which they're lying. Their faces are turned towards me, chalky blurs in the twilight except for the silver gleams of the girl's nose rings. A growl sounds from underneath them as the bull terrier shifts its bulk.

'Stay, Rosie!' the girl hisses, and stupidly I stop. Stand quite still. Rooted to the spot. Until I feel their eyes on me, glaring, so I make a show of rearranging my scarf and buttoning the coat up to my chin before braving the world outside. I have my birthday shoes – they'll carry me home safely enough.

Next morning I get up late. Dark rain runs like spittle down the windows; the trees whine in the wind. I know I'll have to trudge round to the deli again for one of their sugar-glazed *pains aux raisins*. When I was pregnant with Michael, I developed a lifelong craving for raisins, which always grows worse during weather like this.

The shop assistant smiles on seeing me enter with my big, black, man's umbrella. 'The usual, is it, Mrs Harrower?' she asks. 'Something sweet for a dreich day?'

'Oh yes, please.' I smile back, then watch her pick out the largest of the pastries. 'At the rate I eat them, you'd think life was all dreichness …' I finish with a little shrug and the assistant gives the required chuckle as she rings up the till.

The *Herald & Post* is waiting on the doormat, faintly damp. I place it on the kitchen radiator while I grind some luxury-roast coffee beans from Brazil (bought yesterday after my phone call with Michael, on the spur of a sentimental moment). By the time the cafetière is ready, the newspaper has crisped up again and I carry everything through to the living room, where I settle in my favourite armchair.

Then I open the paper, saving the personal ads for last, as a treat. I can spend hours guessing at the real people behind the words, imagining how the 'romantic, fun-and-nature-loving academic in his prime' who wishes to meet 'slim, intelligent blonde between 30 and 35' might actually be a divorced teacher of retirement age with a penchant for hiking and watching sunsets among clouds of midges. I grin to myself, savouring the bitterness of the coffee on my tongue. As I glance through the pages, I uncoil my *pain aux raisins* and tear off bite-sized chunks. The raisins have a slightly burnt taste today, as if the baker had forgotten his pastries in the oven and only just managed to rescue them.

And all of a sudden I hear myself say, 'Enough simply isn't enough, Rosie – it's too little. Too little bustle, too little company, too little sunshine. Not much of a life.'

I'm still swallowing the soft snake-belly centre of the pastry when I find myself standing by the phone, clutching a page of the newspaper. My index finger has started to tap out a number and I can't seem to make it stop: I am ringing a removal firm.

A removal firm?

The advertisement must have caught my attention unawares – or 'subconsciously', as Michael would have said – because it's so big, a third of a page nearly, and has two happily grinning stickmen balancing whole tables and beds on the palms of their hands. One's even got a birdcage on his head. *Silly old bird, silly old bird*, an inner voice cautions me. But with a chortling sense of release I realise that, yes, that's what I want. I want to go off. Want to go away.

'Caledonian Removals, Moira speaking, what's the name and address, please?'

I give her the details: the size of the flat, number of bedrooms, types of furniture, special items like pictures and plants and the dusty old spinning wheel I inherited from my mother, valuables, breakables, the lot. I'm beginning to enjoy myself. *I'm going to go off. I'm going to go away. Michael will be amazed.*

But then the woman inquires about my new address and her question brings me down to earth with a vengeance. I have to go *somewhere*. Going in itself isn't enough. I need a destination. An aim. Always this word. It drove me away from home when I was only eighteen. Drove me all over Switzerland, via France to England and finally to Scotland – and into Jim's eager, grabbing arms. Drove me to become who I am. *Aim. Aim. Aim.*

'Aim high, Rosie. Don't lower your sights unless you have to. Remember that,' my father's teacherly voice used to exhort me. A stern man, despite the sweet smell of his pipe. Leaning forward in his padded leather chair until I'd nod.

So now, on an impulse, I reply with girlish airiness, 'Oh, didn't I mention it? I'm going abroad.'

Instead of asking, 'Where abroad?' which I expect and dread for I really have no idea, the woman says briskly, 'Sorry, we don't do abroad. You'd better try elsewhere. Continental –'

She has started to sound impatient, and I don't blame her. Though perhaps she is merely jealous of me. Perhaps she has children who still need their mother. Still need fed and clothed and sheltered. Need their beds. Their little chests of drawers and trunks spilling toys all over the floor. Their Play Stations, their iPods, their clutter.

After hanging up, I slowly move into the centre of the room and lift my arms for an invisible partner to hold me. I shuffle my feet to the melody of an old-fashioned waltz. I can hear it quite clearly in my head.

Sheena Blackhall

I tend to think of myself as a writer, not a gender. However, many years ago I was interviewed for a chapter in *Sleeping With Monsters* by R.E. Wilson (Polygon 1990), a study of female Celtic poets. When it was published, many writers mentioned their 'muse'. Just as male writers perceive their muse to be female, I perceive mine to be male. Writing empowers me, and gives me a feeling of dominance and control, in a way that I do not experience the world when I am engaged in daily life as a woman.

I am aware that I am lucky, as a female, to live in Scotland. I have travelled in India, Egypt, Ceylon and China, and women in Eastern or Middle Eastern countries have a very different status to that accorded to them here. When my son accompanied me in these countries, it was noticeable that men addressed themselves to him, whereas I became invisible, slightly above the level of chattel, although with one exception I was always treated with courtesy (age has its benefits in the Far East). As a Scot I am interested in the Past, in Nature, in Spirituality. In my case this manifests itself as Buddhism, hence the desire to see it in operation abroad.

It is, of course, easier to pursue an itinerant writing career, as a man. There is generally a partner who stays at home to pay the bills, feed the cat/children and answer the mail, whilst the 'significant other' is free to travel the country giving readings and taking up residencies. I have known one woman who walked away from security to relocate and take up an Artist's residency, and she struggled. Such 'sinecures' are often poorly paid and certainly do not stretch to maintaining two households. My 'comfort zone' is writing, and though I occasionally travel to study other cultures, it is as a child peering in through the window of a shop. You can't take the whole shop home with you. As the Buddha said … it's easier to wear sandals, than to cover the road with leather!

http://screivins.blogspot.com

Sheena Blackhall

Damaged Goods

The urban trees staun sterk, alane,
Up till their queats in gowden smush
An ilkie blatterin, bowfin win
Gars mair leaves birl in the doonrush

The Xmas lichts bleeze in the air
The greasy cassies skyte wi rain
The bus is thrang wi oot-gaun fowk
Grey tears blear ilkie windae-pane

Dowped in ma seat I'm settin oot:
A ceilidh, friens, a festive oor
I'm diddlin a gleg strathspey
An takk nae tent o Winter's clour

A hoodie dichts its vampire beak
Doon its funereal flappin duds
A bairn in wellies stauns ootby
Wytes fur the bus in puils o dubs

I staun an ring the bell tae stop
The driver, bit some gyte granma
Steps on the road. He brakes an sae
A duntit aipple, doon I faa

I think on orchards as a bairn
I stood aneth, the sweet fruit caught
An on the windfaas in the wid
That rummled bruised, an didna stot

Ae meenit, wheeplin a tune,
The neist, I'm laired, heid on the grun
Somelike the rowin o a pirn
It stitches steeked, its threid ootrun.

Sheena Blackhall

The Gas Mask

A gas mask lived in our cupboard
Rubber, with huge bug eyes

Its arrival pre-dated mine,
A female baby-boomer

It belonged with the aerial song
Of bombs that gralloched my city
The thin, high Sirens' whine

Its straps and buckle were tentacles
A disenfranchised horror, clammy's a skylark
Turning sour in the wet clay
It had out-stayed its welcome

At night, in post-war pyjamas
Watching the coal on the fire with its tigers' eyes
I thought of the lungs of soldiers, frothy as candyfloss
Their tongues like those of nightingales, impaled on spits.
A present out of the blue from poisoned skies.

Curriculum for Excellence

I'm a real top-teen in the day's Academy
A confident individual, that's me.
See on a bus? I hae tae be seen
Tae be believed.

I can clear the deck in meenits,
Spittin doon semmits...
Takk Sleepin Beauty yonner
Mebbe she's deid.
Divn't auld fowk gie ye the scunner?
She'd wauken if I skelp her on the heid

I happy-slap a pensioner a day.
Nae my wyte, Missus Social Wirker Thinggy
See, naebody iver showed me foo tae play.
(This is the cue fur aa ye bams tae greet)

Bit I'm a successful learner
An effective contributor tae mayhem, communal keech.

I am tomorrow's citizen, by the way
Interactin in fitbaa stooshies
Touchin up barmaids' titties
Problem solvin foo tae brakk ma ASBO
Spikkin ma wye roon panels
Coontin ma chored gear
Sharin ma stash o hash
Wi the second year

Explorin wyes tae scarifee the warld
(It's social enterprise). Ay, Turner Gallery,
My graffiti's art.
I ken ma richts ... ye canna touch me pal
I'm nae feart o some auld mingin fart

Hit back, I'll say that yer a paedophile
Here ... let me kick yer coupon
Takk it wi a smile.

Susan Sellers

I am an interloper in this book. I am not Scottish and I no longer live here, though I have been employed by a Scottish institution for twelve years, and I did have a home for almost a decade in Cellardyke in the East Neuk of Fife. Like most English people I have Scottish ancestors, and my only child was born at Ninewells Hospital in Dundee – though I appreciate that these facts count for little in these days of diaspora. My main credential for inclusion in this volume is that I continue to work for the University of St Andrews as a Professor of English and Related Literature, even though much of my work now (I went part-time five years ago) revolves around writing and the management of scholarly research projects, such as the Cambridge University Press edition of the writings of Virginia Woolf. Indeed, it is as a virtual Scot that my claim to appear in this volume is strongest, for every one of the many dozen emails I send out each day is automatically headed by the distinctive red and blue St Andrews University shield and concluded by its address. Many of the people with whom I correspond live in geographically distant parts of the world, so it doesn't seem preposterous to respond to queries about the weather with an informed guess that it is likely to be much the same in St Andrews as at my current address in the Fens.

My move south of the border had nothing to do with Scotland itself, though it had everything to do with being a woman and writing. My husband is a composer and an academic in Cambridge, and after years of to-ing and fro-ing we finally faced up to the fact that we needed to settle in one place. Our decision that I should reduce my post and return south rather than the other way round was motivated by my desire to have more time with my child and to write. It seems fitting that my first novel, *Vanessa and Virginia* (a tale about Virginia Woolf and the painter Vanessa Bell), is published in Britain by a Scottish Press, Two Ravens.

Scottish? What's That?

It never occurred to me that it was a different country. After all, Scotland and England have been joined since the Act of Union in 1707, part of the United Kingdom. We speak the same language, use the same currency. I'd worked abroad, in Paris, Swaziland, South America – places where my foreignness was highlighted no matter how adept I became at fitting in. It wouldn't be like that in Scotland. So when Douglas Dunn – then Head of English at the University of St Andrews – rang and offered me a post I accepted without a second's hesitation. I did have a slight wobble as I headed up the M6 towards Carlisle after a full day of driving past signs that still pointed resolutely 'North'. I had started my journey on the Dorset/Hampshire border and was beginning to wonder how much further 'north' it was possible to go. There was nothing significant about the border itself. I saw a sign, welcoming motorists to Scotland, but given the speed at which I was travelling if I had blinked I would have missed it. Certainly there were no border guards, no checking of papers or monitoring of vehicles to mark the transition to a different land.

St Andrews, when I finally got there, did little to dislodge my complacency. Market Street had all the usual shops in it, albeit in a slightly reduced form. Though I heard the soft lilt of Scottish accents as I waited in the queue for the checkout at Boots, it felt no more alien than the Brummy drawl of the attendants in the service station I had stopped at somewhere near Wolverhampton. Even the meaning of the odd unusual word – hen, blether, snippy – was immediately apparent from its context and served only to add a local charm. After all, London – where I had spent the summer – has a rich and varied vocabulary all its own. The place I chose for lunch turned out to be full of American golfers, giving the town a cosmopolitan air.

Any differences, during my first weeks in Fife, remained firmly within the category of the quaint. There was the landlady who refused me a room when she discovered that my partner and I were unmarried. Even my assurances that we were engaged could not assuage her sense that our liaison was somehow sinful.

There was also a visit to the Byre theatre, where in those days tea and shortbread were served from a trolley by an elderly couple wearing matching kilts. One morning I inadvertently parked across an entrance as I stopped at a shop, blocking a car in its drive. I realised my error only some minutes later as I happened to glance out of the window and catch sight of the frustrated driver. I hurried outside to apologise, bracing myself for the peal of angry expletives I was sure were coming. Imagine my astonishment when instead I was greeted with a friendly 'nae worries' and an invitation to 'finish yer messages'. Though the experience cheered me, I did not attribute it to any variation in national culture. If anything, I told myself it was one of the advantages of small town as opposed to urban living. Life in St Andrews happened at a gentler pace than in the metropolis I had come from.

Often, I found it hard to remember that I was in Scotland at all. There was the time I needed to phone a prospective Italian exchange student from the main office. The person who answered spoke in Italian and in order to impress upon her the fact that my call was long-distance I told her 'I was phoning from England'. The secretary – who had noticed my faux-pas – did not say a word as I returned the phone to her desk. Not everything was rosy. There were misunderstandings and disagreements. One evening, visiting a colleague in Crail, I offered to make moussaka and called in at a grocer's to buy aubergines. The shopkeeper looked at me sharply. 'There's no call for that sort of thing round here,' she admonished. Then there was the taxi driver who mistook a comment about the colours of the autumn leaves and assured me that if he had his way all roadside trees would be felled. I realised I had stumbled across one of those types who revere concrete. Not for a moment did I imagine that, because I was no longer in London where every tree seems a cause for rejoicing, I had finally encountered a common Scottish trait. People are people after all.

The day the Scots played England at rubgy was a little harder to wear, but then I was never that interested in sport. As I gazed at the flags that suddenly appeared in windows, I reminded myself that something similar happened all over Britain, whenever the local team played at home. On the whole, I finished my first semester at St Andrews with the sense that any oddities I had encountered were those of a new situation, not a foreign culture.

The change came when my partner and I decided to buy a house. We couldn't afford St Andrews so we moved to Cellardyke, a small fishing village on the East Neuk of Fife about twelve miles away. The accents here were harsher – this was the first time I heard the word 'haar' – and as we put our key into our new front door I was aware of curious glances. I had lived in small communities before and made a point of introducing myself to our immediate neighbours. That afternoon, as we stood on the beach opposite our house and watched the sea pound the harbour wall, shooting fountains of spray into the air, we felt we had arrived in a corner of paradise.

I was conscious of fresh stares as I left for work the next morning. The only person I spoke to was a woman hanging her washing on the communal clothes lines on the harbour walkway, but I could tell from the twitching of curtains and the sudden removal of milk bottles from doorsteps that I was being observed. The woman – who introduced herself as Elsie – commented on my briefcase and asked where I worked, then told me of an Icelandic resident in the village as well as a German woman she thought I might like. Though I smiled to myself at her unspoken implication that the people I would have most in common with were foreigners, I appreciated her friendliness. My brief morning conversations with Elsie became a regular feature, and one I always looked forward to.

Then I did something to alter all this. It was not in the grand scheme of things anything very revolutionary – I made a few improvements to the front of the house, added some tubs of flowers – but it was an innovation. Eddie, the sour old man who routinely parked slammed up against the sitting room window, was obliged to park a few yards further away. He was outraged; suddenly the village was his. Eddie was born on the harbour, I had merely bought a house there. This was the first time I was called an 'incomer' to my face. The fact that I was a working woman counted against me too. Whereas before, my post at the University had been a source of conversation, now it served to confirm that I was only an interloper in a community where I had no indigenous rights. I was branded, aggressively, as 'English', and I sensed that from this moment on whatever I did or said would be viewed in this light – as if my nationality were a cloak that had suddenly become visible.

Time passed and the new became familiar. The following summer I noticed other residents putting flower pots outside their doors. A house on the other side of the harbour that had stood empty was bought by a young family and attention switched to them. Enmities and alliances shifted, as, for example, in the year when the sea brought part of the harbour wall down and Eddie and I found ourselves fighting on the same side. This time our 'enemy' was Fife County Council and their team of contracted builders, as the village struggled to accommodate the large-scale engineering works the breach in the harbour wall caused.

I left Fife in the Spring of 2003 to return to England. When I look back on my time in Cellardyke now, I realise that I was given a practical lesson in human relationships. Differences we can usually accommodate, especially when we have a common enemy or aim. What causes dissension is our fear of the unknown.

There is a codicil to this story. My son was born while I lived in Fife. I became mother to a Scot. When he was five I took him to a friend's wedding in England, dressed – at his request – in a kilt. My son is football-crazy and boasted to my friend that one day he hoped to play for Scotland. I smiled; personally I didn't mind which team he supported as long as he was happy. My friend smiled too. 'Good for you,' she encouraged. Then she turned to me. 'Great Scottish accent!' I hadn't even noticed.

Copyright information

Train Notes 2007: Edinburgh–Leuchars–Dundee © Kirsty Gunn and Meaghan Delahunt; *A Glaswegian in Orkney; North Ronaldsay; When you leave; Wish I had…* © Pamela Beasant; *Excision/ As Long as I Can Stay Here* © Celaen Chapman; *Dream Waker; Yesterday's Man* © Alison Craig; *Two Sides* © Alison Flett; *Highland Girl* © Jackie Kay; *Night Walk; Caesarian* © Sylvia Hays; *'What Kept You?'* © Erica Munro; *Co-op Funeral Parlour; First Love* © Gerda Stevenson; *Oh Brother* © Agnes Owens; *The Island Folk/Das Inselvolk* © Dilys Rose; *Last Train To Ayr, Saturday 24th March 2007; Tasting Stars* © Sheila Templeton; *Walking the Parapets* © Anne Macleod; *Home Truths; Motherland; What Does it Mean to be a Woman Living in Scotland?; Smothering Words* © Dorothy Baird; *Breaking Stones* © Anne Morrison; *Passage Migrant* © Elizabeth Reeder; *The Long Missing* © Cynthia Rogerson; *Refuge; scotland* © Janet Paisley; *Stac Jenny* © Alison Napier; *Grey; Elvis's jacket* © Laureen Johnson; *The Invisible Women of Scotland; Survivor; Mrs MacGrundy* © Joy Hendry; *Being Forty; Paper Daughter; carry carry life finish* © Mandy Haggith; *Aschenputtel 07* © Lesley McDowell; *Talisman; Scottish Woman* © Patricia Ace; *This Side of Heaven* © Laura Marney; *St Magnus Festival Poet; Yggdrasil* © Yvonne Gray; *Cailliche* © Linda Cracknell; *Here; Listen* © Sharon Blackie; *On the Run* © Margaret Elphinstone; *A' Bheatha na Rìomhachas Suarach; Life in her Glad-Rags* © Meg Bateman; *The Direction of One's Gaze; Balancing Equations* © Morag MacInnes; *Deep; "CRUMBS!"; Gone; The Uncovering; Trapped* © Pauline Prior-Pitt; *Invisible Partners* © Regi Claire; *Damaged Goods; The Gas Mask; Curriculum for Excellence* © Sheena Blackhall; *Scottish? What's That?* © Susan Sellers

Two Ravens Press titles by writers in 'Cleave'

Fiction

The Long Delirious Burning Blue
Sharon Blackie

'It is that rarity, a first novel that smacks of not merely confidence, but authority, a sense that the story is true and clearly envisioned, with the technique to make it seem seamless, dynamic and written with verve and a care for the English language ... The ending is powerful (reminiscent of The English Patient*), filmic, and achieving the kind of symmetry that novels often aspire to, but rarely reach.'* ***Tom Adair, The Scotsman***

'... Hugely potent. A tribute to the art of storytelling that is itself an affecting and inspiring story.' ***The Independent on Sunday***

'... a cleverly-woven presentation of how violence and lies within a family work down the generations.'
Scottish Review of Books

'Sharon Blackie writes with a real sense of truth and emotional depth about relationships between individuals, and between individuals and their environment. Her characters are figures in a landscape brought vividly, vibrantly to life.' ***Nicholas Royle***

£8.99. ISBN 978-1-906120-17-7. Published February 2008.

The Last Bear
Mandy Haggith

'The Last Bear *is as much poem as prose, a lament for the last bear in Scotland, and the human ways of life that died with her. With the imposition of an alien religion the old harmonies are disrupted; the last bear is the final sacrifice of the old order.* The Last Bear *focuses on a pivotal historical moment, yet the results echo on down the centuries: the pain and loss of* The Last Bear *is, in fact, our own.'* ***Margaret Elphinstone***

£8.99. ISBN 978-1-906120-16-0. Published March 2008

Love Letters from my Death-bed
Cynthia Rogerson

'Rogerson's prose has a wonderful energy and rhythm. She is a master storyteller whose love of language and black humour

envelops the reader within the strange and strangely familiar, sometimes reminiscent of early John Irving. A delightfully funny and often deeply touching book.'
Laura Hird, Scottish Review of Books

'...a comedy of manners, a contemporary romp focused on death and love in a chaotic, cynical world. Rogerson's deft prose laces each scene with light.' **Anne Macleod, Northwords Now**

£8.99. ISBN 978-1-906120-00-9. Published April 2007

Vanessa and Virginia
Susan Sellers

'A beautiful, haunting novel about the love, the rivalry between two gifted sisters, and the real purpose of Art. The achievement here is an uncanny, utterly persuasive empathy for both sisters, and the world and times in which they lived.'
John Burnside

'Deftly, apparently effortlessly, Susan Sellers's novel of love, art, and sexual jealousy gives us convincing and intimate access to the relationship between two remarkable sisters. At once pellucid and sophisticated, Vanessa and Virginia *is quite simply a pleasure to read.'* **Robert Crawford**

£8.99. ISBN 978-1-906120-27-6. Published June 2008

Poetry

Castings
Mandy Haggith

'The poetry here shows real clarity of eye marking the dialogues of nature in a place, be that place the lonely Scottish crofting area that is home, or the course of the River Kelvin through the Lowlands, or a Russian forest.' **Tom Leonard**

'Outstanding originality and quality. Impressive for its sharpness, sympathy and decisiveness...' **Alan Riach**

£8.99. ISBN 978-1-906120-01-6. Published April 2007

Leaving the Nest
Dorothy Baird

'These pieces are the outpouring of a remarkable talent... In an increasingly ugly and unpredictable world, these poems are

a reminder and an example of just how beautiful life can be.' ***Christopher Rush***

£8.99. ISBN 978-1-906120-06-1. Published July 2007

Running With a Snow Leopard

Pamela Beasant

'...breathtakingly evocative detail...unabashed spontaneity – and sheer musicality.' ***Stewart Conn***

'Pam Beasant writes about landscape ... in such palpable terms that you can feel the particular light of the curious conversation she so eloquently describes between sea and sky, sea and land, sea, sky and land (because all are quite different) in such a way that you feel you are there. She writes ... with intrinsic purity – and, more importantly, simple craft, so that we see into her life as a mirror of our own ...' ***Joy Hendry***

£8.99. ISBN 978-1-906120-14-6. Published January 2008

In The Hanging Valley

Yvonne Gray

'Yvonne Gray's poems represent a taut lyric of images, people and places. Here is a poet who is aware of the tensions and nuances which make up the modern world, but behind it there is an awareness of a more ancient acoustic: one which makes us who we are.' ***George Gunn***

'Yvonne Gray's poems breathe with the air of Orkney ...one can detect the musician's ear in her writing. Her poems stitch images into a fabric: one rich and textured but at the same time light and unshowy ...With words she paints the picture, the music.' ***Christine De Luca***

£8.99. ISBN 978-1-906120-19-1. Published March 2008
